The **UNIVERSAL** Library

THE
American Presidency

THE PATTEN FOUNDATION

Mr. Will Patten of Indianapolis (A.B., Indiana University, 1893) made in 1931 a gift for the establishment of the Patten Foundation at his Alma Mater. Under the terms of this gift, which became available upon the death of Mr. Patten (May 3, 1936), there is to be chosen each year a Visiting Professor who is to be in residence several weeks during the year. The purpose of this prescription is to provide an opportunity for members of the University, students and faculty to enjoy the privilege and advantage of personal acquaintance with the Visiting Professor. The Visiting Professor for the Patten Foundation in 1938-1939 was

PROFESSOR HAROLD J. LASKI
London School of Economics and Political Science
University of London

HAROLD J. LASKI

THE

American Presidency

AN INTERPRETATION

The Universal Library

GROSSET & DUNLAP

NEW YORK

BY ARRANGEMENT WITH HARPER & BROTHERS

CONTENTS

*

PREFACE

IN THE spring of 1939 Indiana University hon-
ored me with an invitation to lecture there on the
Patten Foundation; this volume is, substantially, the
course I delivered. I should like to thank President
H. B Wells for an experience as stimulating as it was
delightful. I should add that, in their printed form,
these pages owe much to the discussions I had in
Bloomington with many members of the faculty, and,
in particular, to my friends Dean Bernard Gavit, and
Professors Ford Hall and Fowler Harper. I shall long
remember their kindness, and that of Mr. S. Yellen
and Mr. Harry Engel.

This book is, as its subtitle seeks to indicate, less a
treatise on the presidency of the United States than
an attempt, made through English eyes, to interpret
the way in which it actually works. I am, I hope, sufficiently aware of the dangers to which any student
is exposed who seeks to explain a foreign institution.
I can only plead that there is a sense in which I have
been watching the presidency at work, sometimes
from near at hand, ever since I began to teach at
Harvard nearly twenty-five years ago; and there are
few of the arguments I have ventured to put forward
that have not had the benefit of criticism from many
American friends, both academic and political.

Its errors are, of course, all my own. But I should indeed be ungrateful if I did not acknowledge the immense debt it owes for what merit it may possess to those friends. In particular, its obligation to Mr. Justice Frankfurter and to Dr. Alfred E. Cohn is quite beyond my power of repayment.

I owe much, too, to some of the standard works on the subject. In particular, I should like to mention how much I have been helped by the writings of Professors Lindsay Rogers, Charles Beard, and Thomas Reed Powell. I found also immense assistance in the elaborate investigation of Professor Dangerfield into the relation of the Senate to the treaty-making power. I should add that the biographies and autobiographies of leading American statesmen, above all the superb *Diary* of John Quincy Adams, as abridged by Allan Nevins from the *Memoirs*, are an indispensable source of understanding.

American scholars have done so much, especially in recent years, for the study of English institutions, that I hope this little book may stimulate British students to realize something of the interest and fascination of American history and politics. If it does this even in a small degree, it will not have been written wholly in vain.

H. J. L.

Little Bardfield,
  Essex.

I

INTRODUCTORY

I

INSTITUTIONS are living things, and they do not easily yield their secrets to the printed word. Predominantly, that is not because they are in themselves mysterious. It is rather because they change with changes in the environment within which they operate, and partly because they differ, from one moment to the other, in terms of the men who operate them. The premiership of Great Britain was one thing in the hands of Mr. Lloyd George in time of war; it was a different thing in the hands of Mr. Baldwin in time of peace; it is a different thing, again, in the hands of Mr. Neville Chamberlain. So, too, with the presidency of France. Though the books warn us that here is the one head of a state whose constant characteristic is that he neither reigns nor governs, in fact, the office has been very different in the hands of its various holders; notably it has hardly seemed the same thing in the hands of M. Poincaré as what it has been in the hands of M. Doumergue.

No important institution, moreover, is ever merely what the law makes it. It accumulates about itself traditions, conventions, ways of behavior, which, without ever attaining the status of formal law, are not less formidable in their influence than law itself could require. The prerogatives of the Crown in Great Britain are perhaps the supreme example of this habit; many of them retain their formal status as law and yet could hardly be revived without what would amount to a constitutional revolution. The habits of one period, this is to say, can hardly hope to determine the conduct of its successor. The dynamics of life require a continuity of adaptation which almost always means that the formal appearance is different, at any given moment, from the actual reality. To penetrate that reality, therefore, is always a difficult matter. In part, it is obscured, as most institutional phenomena are obscured, by the complexity of the material itself. The processes of government are very like an iceberg; what appears on the surface may be but a small part of the reality beneath. How difficult it is to judge that reality is well known to every historian. Even those most closely concerned in the processes may totally misjudge their meaning. Both the king of France and the tsar of Russia wholly failed to grasp the events, respectively, of 1789 and 1917; and Mr. Asquith's resignation, in December, 1916, was intended to lead to the elimination, and not to the triumph, of Mr. Lloyd George.

The observation of institutions is difficult for another reason. No student can fail, consciously or unconsciously, to bring his own scheme of values to them. He may be detached; he cannot hope to be impartial. For he brings to the task of observation not merely the experience in which he is involved—an experience which is bound to color his power to see what is before him. He brings to it, also, his own hopes and fears, his judgment of good and bad, significant and insignificant. And this is more certain to be the case when he seeks to explain an institution which he sees from without. There, he is almost bound to be impressed by what in it is alien from the routine to which he is accustomed. He sees more emphatically the unwonted side than the side which resembles the experience with which he is familiar. More than this. In seeking to understand its operation, he is bound to rely upon the judgment of men who have themselves seen it from within. But they, in their turn, as they describe its working to him, bring to that description a body of assumptions the meaning of which he can grasp only as he is conscious that they are being made. Everyone knows that Gibbon's great history derives a considerable part of its unique character from the fact that its author was a philosophic rationalist of the eighteenth century. Everyone knows, also, how much Sir Henry Maine's judgment of popular government was colored by his years as Legal Member of the Viceroy's Council in India. Even a work like Stubbs's *Constitutional History* was profoundly influenced, as Vinogradoff has pointed out,[1] by the rising tide of Victorian liberalism; and that, be it added, even though its author regarded himself as an orthodox Conservative.

I am to speak, being an Englishman, of the supreme political office in the United States. I am aware of my

[1] *Villainage in England* (1892), Preface.

temerity. But to emphasize my sense that the adventure is a delicate one, I should like to give one more example of what I mean by the influence of one's environment upon the judgment. Save perhaps the *Democracy in America* of de Tocqueville, no more famous book on that theme has been written than Bryce's *American Commonwealth*; from the moment of its appearance, just over fifty years ago, it at once took its place as a work of classic quality. Its author was already an eminent historian and a jurist of exceptional distinction. He had traveled widely all over the United States. He was intimately acquainted with many of the leading figures in its political and intellectual eye. He had taken more pains to examine the United States, and with greater energy, than any previous observer. Certainly he knew more of the American political scene, when he wrote, than any European, not even excluding de Tocqueville, had previously known.

Yet Bryce was also a Gladstonian Liberal, immersed in the special philosophy represented by that experience. When he came, therefore, to look at the American industrial scene, he viewed its substance, both as to the mind of the labor movement, on the one hand, and as to the relation of labor to the governmental process, on the other, very much with the mental outlook of a Victorian Liberal, who mainly noted the better economic condition of the workingman in America, his ampler margins of opportunity, compared to those enjoyed by the workingman in England. He did not examine American trade unions at first hand. He took his view of the problems of law and order created by industrial unrest either from the political figures whom he met at Washington, or from political journals, like the *Nation* then edited by his friend Godkin, which accepted a social philosophy akin to his own. The result was that he hardly knew how profound was the American labor problem in his day; and nearly every judgment he made about its influence on governmental policy has subsequently been called into question by later historical investigation. He was wholly wide of the mark in his judgment of the Haymarket riot;[2] he knew nothing of the inner and dubious details which went to the making of Cleveland's decision to aid the railroads;[3] even the revised edition of 1910 takes no account of the existence of the American Federation of Labor.[4] His revised edition was made two years before the great upheaval of 1912 and the famous Pujo Committee of 1913.[5] Yet he has no knowledge of the Populist movement except as an incident in the Democratic party's acceptance of a free silver policy in 1896. He is not aware of the degree to which Populism looks backward in its implications to the first political struggles of the republic, or forward to that Roosevelt epoch in which so many of the outlines of contemporary controversies began to emerge. Of the great strikes led by the Knights of

[2] *American Commonwealth* (ed. of 1911), II, 646. Cf. Henry David, *The History of the Haymarket Affair* (1936), and Samuel Yellen, *American Labor Struggles* (1936), Chap. II.

[3] *Ibid.*, II, 599. Cf. Yellen, *op. cit.*, Chap. IV.

[4] Trade unions do not even appear in the index to his book.

[5] On the Pujo Committee see L. D. (Mr. Justice) Brandeis, *Other People's Money* (1915).

Labor on the railroads, he can write that "when recently a gigantic organization of workingmen, purporting to unite the whole of American labor, attempted to enforce its sentences against particular firms or corporations by a boycott in which all laborers were urged to join, there was displeasure, but no panic, no call for violent remedies. The prevailing faith in liberty and in the good sense of the mass was unshaken; and the result soon justified this tranquil faith."[6]

There is hardly a phrase in these sentences that would stand examination today;[7] and they are not less revealing for their underlying assumptions than they are for their factual inaccuracies. Bryce accepted the simple faith in liberty of contract as between individual employer and individual worker that was characteristic of his time; and he had no conception that its implications were largely obsolete even when he wrote the first edition of his book. He brought with him to America, in a word, a social philosophy, a way of life, that set the criteria not only of what he was to look for, but also of what he found. He mingled in America almost wholly with the same type of men he was accustomed to meet in England—college presidents, statesmen, editors, bankers, and eminent industrialists; men, that is to say, who shared, overwhelmingly, his own point of view. It is not, therefore, surprising that his judgment of what he ought to look for in America was confirmed by them; or

[6] *Op. cit.*, II, 646.
[7] Cf. *op. cit.* Yellen.

[6]

that, very largely, his judgment of what he found was their judgment. Bryce was a disinterested and detached observer, if ever there was one. Yet his account of what he saw is, in this particular context, a striking example of how the subconscious personal equation is vital in the conclusions at which even a disinterested and detached observer will arrive.

I use the illustration of Bryce's book because it shows how careful one must be in seeking to estimate, especially as an Englishman, an institution so intricate and, I add, psychologically unfamiliar, as the American presidency. Part of its functions are like those of the British Crown; part of them can be made to appear like those of the British prime minister; and the temptation is great to think of them in these terms. Yet it is fundamental to remember that, in each part, the resemblances are far less striking than the differences, and that the functioning of the institution as a whole results in the unique consequences which cannot be predicted when those parts are separately surveyed. It is not, I think, merely a platitude to say that the essence of the presidency is the fact that it is an *American* institution, that it functions in an American environment, that it has been shaped by the forces of American history, that it must be judged by American criteria of its response to American needs. To us in England, for example, it appears wholly wasteful that, after the immense experience the tenure of such an office confers, only one American president should have been able to utilize it in political life after his term had expired. (The brief senatorial service of Andrew

Johnson hardly counts.) Yet the whole ethos of the American political system would be different if that were not the case; and to argue, for example, that Americans ought to have a House of Lords in which ex-presidents can function usefully is to miss the vital fact that the very nature of American politics prevents either house of Congress from functioning in any way like the House of Lords.

Englishmen, again, are tempted to remark on the fact that many of the presidents of the United States have been very ordinary men, not to be distinguished from several millions of their fellows; Lord Bryce has a chapter in his book entitled "Why Great Men Do Not Become Presidents." But the judgment, I suggest, is a facile one. On any showing, eleven American presidents have been extraordinary men, whatever may be our view of the handling of their office. That is a proportion not less high than the proportion of remarkable men who have become prime minister in the same period; and, among those who could not be judged extraordinary, two at least, Tyler and Polk, seem on the evidence that has now accumulated to have been at least as fit for the office they held as were, say, Sir Henry Campbell-Bannerman or Mr. Bonar Law for the office of prime minister. A foreigner may distrust the methods by which the president is chosen; certainly there is a good deal of truth in Bagehot's famous aphorism, apropos of Lincoln, that "success in a lottery is no argument for lotteries." But, of course, the assumption of his remark is that the choice of Lincoln in 1860 was an accident. That is not the case. Few choices have ever been more carefully or-

ganized in a presidential convention. It is true that
Lincoln was nationally known only a short time before his nomination. But it is worth remembering that
Mr. Baldwin was hardly known at all when he became
prime minister, and that, so far, each Labour leader
in England, with only one exception, has been chosen
as a result of a series of fortuitous circumstances none
of which was foreseen. And it is far from rare in our
party history to find that the prime minister is less
the obvious man than the most available man. We train
our leaders differently, and we keep them longer. But
we must not transfer the criteria of our own system
to that of the United States without a care greater
than we usually exercise.

A good deal, in fact, of the literature upon American institutions applies to the standards derived from
European experience. That is true, it is worth while to
add, even of much that has been written by Americans themselves. The classic work of Woodrow Wilson, for example, would hardly have come to some of
its conclusions—that on the procedure of the Senate,
for instance—if its author had not been steeped in
Burke and Bagehot and had not seen a good deal of
American government through their eyes. We compare the long political career of an English prime
minister with the brevity of that of an American president; but the true comparison is surely between the
periods in which each held the highest office in the
state, and, if we make that comparison, more American presidents have held office for eight years than
have British prime ministers since the younger Pitt.

We speak of the long apprenticeship to politics that an English prime minister serves before he reaches 10 Downing Street; we forget, I think, not only that American conditions altogether rule out (I do not think wisely) that kind of apprenticeship, but also that, in the postwar years in England, the apprenticeship we have come to regard as habitual has been notably abridged in time.

Older commentators, again, and, especially Bagehot, complained of the poor quality of political writing in the American newspapers as compared with that in the English press; and they attributed this to the influence of the fixed presidential term in the United States as compared with the dramatic elasticity of the English system. Later history has made it possible to doubt this conclusion. For the increasing rigidity of the English party structure, on the one hand, and the decline of importance, especially in the postwar years, of the editorial page, on the other, have combined with the reduction of the press to a department of big business to give it, except in moments of gravest emergency, far less importance in its influence on political decisions than was true in Bagehot's day. In America, however, while the influence of the editorial page has continued to decline, there has been the rise of the independent political commentator whose articles probably have a more far-reaching influence than the work of any English editors, and whose status in American public life is comparable with that of Delane in the most important days of the London *Times*. The reasons for these developments are complicated; but one of them, at least, is the fact that party structure in the United States remains far less rigid than in Great Britain and the influence of the independent voter, influenced in his turn by the political commentator, is far greater. There are many journals in the United States the columns of which are mainly studied for articles of this kind. They shape the climate of American opinion very much as does the work of the great English cartoonist, David Low. They build a stereotype of ideas which slowly, but incisively, makes its impact upon those who shape decisions in Washington.

Any discussion, therefore, of so essentially American an institution as the presidency must seek to analyze its working in American terms. Whatever the intention of the founders, the history of the United States has molded it in ways they could not have foreseen; and its ways of behavior, the criteria by which it is to be judged, must be set by the conditions in which it has to work. There is no foreign institution with which, in any basic sense, it can be compared, because, basically, there is no comparable foreign institution. The president of the United States is both more and less than a king; he is, also, both more and less than a prime minister. The more carefully his office is studied, the more does its unique character appear. We are, indeed, entitled to criticize the results of its operation; and, particularly, we can compare those results with the consequences which follow from the operation of other systems. But we must constantly bear in mind that the transplantation of methods from other countries to American soil would, in all human probability, produce results quite different from any which their advocates have been inclined to anticipate; after all, the British parliamentary system has been different in each country of its adoption, just as American federation has undergone a decisive sea-change with its transference to other climes. Not the least danger in the study of politics is the attempt to construct large generalizations which flow from the comparison of two unlikes, on the ground that the institutions involved have a similar part to play in the respective governmental systems. The more fully we avoid generalizations of this character, the more likely we are to understand the nature of the material with which we have to deal.

2

No one who studies the proceedings of the constitutional convention can fail to see one emphasis in its construction of the presidency which has remained a living part of the traditions in which it is imbedded. Fear of executive despotism is, for reasons intelligible enough in the light of American origins, evoked in the public approach to the office. Though Lincoln and Woodrow Wilson both exercised, in the pressure of wartime conditions, an almost dictatorial power, it is, I think, true to say that each wielded it with uneasiness; and the exercise of that power was in each case followed by a strong reaction toward congressional control of presidential action. It is not, I suggest, accident that for twenty years after Lincoln there was no strong president until Cleveland; and that the twelve years after Woodrow Wilson saw the effective leadership of American policy outside the White House. For the first few months of his period of office, President Franklin Roosevelt dominated both houses of Congress; but it is notable that, after the summer of 1933, the development of congressional challenge to his authority mounted constantly in volume.

The reasons for this are, I suspect, threefold in character. Partly, they lie in the constitutional position of the office itself. The president is at no point the master of the legislature. He can indicate a path of action to Congress. He can argue, bully, persuade, cajole; but he is always outside Congress, and subject to a will he cannot dominate. He is, while in office, the national leader of his party; of set purpose, he is not, and cannot be, its congressional leader. Even if his party has a majority in both houses, he has to win the good will of his party in Congress; he cannot exact it. A president, indeed, who sought to do so would soon discover the limits of his power. Mr. F. D. Roosevelt was resoundingly beaten on his Court plan shortly after his remarkable triumph of 1936. Successive presidents, since 1920, have recommended in vain the adherence of the United States to the Permanent International Court. The lobby of the American Legion has proved more successful with both houses, ever since the end of the War of 1914, than any pressure, even including the exercise of the veto power, that the president could bring to bear.

He can initiate policy; he cannot control it. The emergency of war apart, that has been the constant characteristic of his position ever since 1789. That was the intent of the founders; and, broadly, it has continued to win the approval, as an intent, of public opinion. If its origin was, as I have said, a natural fear of executive despotism, its continuance must be sought in other directions. Partly, I think, it lies in the nature of American conditions from 1789 until almost the other day. The wide opportunities, the boundless resources, the habits of a frontier civilization, all these made against the idea of a positive state. Americans did not feel they needed strong government. They felt, out of an experience which seemed continually to reverify itself, that they could rely upon their own exertions for material advancement. *Ne pas trop gouverner* was the lesson extracted by their business men from their marvelous success in developing the continent. A strong executive meant the risk of interference from Washington. Interference meant a disturbance of the confidence upon which business men depend. Government regulation and business prosperity were deemed—are largely still deemed—mighty opposites. Whenever a strong president—Jackson, Tyler, Theodore Roosevelt, Wilson, Franklin Roosevelt—has been in office, business men have always been alarmed by the tendency of affairs.

"We are," wrote Henry Clay, when Jackson was in office, "in the midst of a revolution, hitherto bloodless, but rapidly leading towards a total change of the pure republican character of the government and to the concentration of all power in the hands of one man. The powers of Congress are paralyzed except when exerted in conformity with his will." Jackson was a strong president; yet no student but is aware how baseless was the view Clay here expressed. Yet it is an attitude which has been taken by men not less able than Clay in each instance when a president of strong will has shown himself in the White House. And so far, in each instance, the constant reiteration of a baseless warning has resulted in the choice of a successor to a strong president who has half-abdicated from the control of policy.

The third reason for this suspicion of the strong executive lies, I believe, in the reasons that have led to his choice. In each case, so far, his election has been the outcome of a popular revolt, more or less conscious, against the business man's dominating influence upon the exercise of political power. Jefferson represented a revolt of the West against the narrow property interests of Eastern Federalism. Jackson embodied the nascent agrarian suspicion of Eastern banking power. Cleveland and Theodore Roosevelt were both, as it were, protest presidents—the one against corruption, and Northern domination of the South; the other against the growth of corporate power. Woodrow Wilson embodied the hostility of the little man to the trusts, his fear of being dominated by the octopus of Wall Street. Franklin Roosevelt was elected, as he himself said, by the "forgotten man," the trade unionist, the worker on relief, the little shopkeeper, the tenant-farmer, the millions, in short, who had abruptly

[15]

discovered the hollowness of the permanent prosperity the Coolidge-Mellon epoch had seemed to foreshadow.

It is notable that the tendency to strong presidents coincides with epochs of difficulty in the United States; it is notable, also, that strong presidents have come with greater frequency in more recent times than in early American history. The reason is the obvious one that, with the exhaustion of frontier conditions, the problems of America have become increasingly the same in essence as those of a typical capitalist democracy in western Europe. No doubt, the economic opportunities are still larger, the social stratification much less intense, the ability to experiment far wider, than in Europe. But there has finally emerged a vast working-class which needs the protection of the state if it is to have security and the minimum conditions of civilized living. There is a vast concentration of wealth in relatively few hands; and there is an increasing centralization of economic power. Every problem in the European scene reproduces itself in the United States; and none of the problems is capable of solution without executive leadership of the political forces involved.

This presents two issues of major magnitude in the context of the presidency. As things are, leadership can come from the president alone; for reasons that I shall discuss later, there is no other source of direction which can secure the attention of the whole nation. But the forces which operate against continuity of presidential leadership are immense. There are the forces inherent in the Constitution—an absolute divi-

sion of powers, a system of checks and balances as between executive and legislative which gives to each an
interest in the diminution of authority instead of in
its consolidation, a tendency to destroy something of
the president's prestige as his first term draws to an
end, and to weaken most of it in the latter part of his
second. There are the forces, secondly, inherent in
the nature of business enterprise—their fear of governmental regulation in general, the timidity and inertia of property before economic innovation, the de-
pressing effect upon business enterprise of the level of
taxation usually implicit in any economic innovation
that comes from government. There are the forces of
the cultural heritage, which always make the relation
between political forms and social needs dispropor-
tionate; a disproportion which is intensified by the
fact that, since a strong president is usually the outcome either of emergency or of profound discontent,
he must usually be spectacularly successful if he is to
maintain increased authority without abridgment. For
increased authority will always meet with resistance
from those whose interest it is to stand by the ancient
ways; and, on the evidence, they will exhaust all their
power and ingenuity to prevent the prospect of any
spectacular success.

It cannot be too often remembered that the founders
of the Constitution were working in a predominantly
agricultural society in which the consequences of the
Industrial Revolution could not be even dimly realized.
They feared the masses. They were adamant about
the "rights" of property. Liberty to them predomi-

nantly meant protection of vested interests from the invasions of the multitude. No one can read the proceedings of the Philadelphia convention without seeing how infinite were the precautions they took against the creation of a presidential office which should lend the color of its personality to the scheme of government. At every point, the limits of its possible operations were narrowly set; and we can see in the *Diary* of Maclay how jealously its activities were watched. History has made it possible for some of these limitations to be transcended. Certainly, the use of the presidency in Franklin Roosevelt's hands would have been unthinkable—Lincoln, perhaps, apart—to any president before Theodore Roosevelt, and even to most of his successors. But the original conception of the office has, both legally and psychologically, profoundly influenced the limits of the direction it may attempt. Every failure in such an attempt causes the pendulum of opinion to swing back to a more negative conception of the office; and, since the positive conception is at once new and exceptional, in the mind of the most powerful class in America there is an almost a priori case against its operation. Men cling tenaciously to their wonted routines. The American people are not yet accustomed to think of the presidency as the essential keystone of the political arch. We have to remember that, as recently as the era of Woodrow Wilson, the office seemed a source of supplement and correction to business control rather than an agency which was to set the pace and direction of the nation's political life.

The grave question of the future is whether it will be able to do so. There are many factors which make this dubious. A president limited by the will of Congress is always like a sailor on an uncharted sea; he cannot proceed with certainty upon his course. There is the problem of winning a renomination, and the price he may have to pay for it. There is the problem of whether a term that, so far, has not exceeded eight years gives time enough, within the character of the system, to implement any full scheme of ideas; a Republican president might easily work havoc with the New Deal, and even a Democratic successor might jeopardize its outstanding features. There is the problem of securing not merely the legislative but also the administrative co-operation he requires. There is the problem, always omnipresent to an innovating president, of the Supreme Court; the accidents of the appointing power have made a good deal of history in the judicial sphere. Even if we grant, as I should at once grant, that a great president today has more chance of having his way than at any previous time in the history of the office, it is still an open question whether the conditions under which the Constitution itself, and the traditions it has imposed, still operate give him the elbowroom he requires for a fully constructive job.

It is not as though, in the American system, the initiative is supplied from elsewhere. For reasons that I shall discuss in another chapter, the Congress is not a body capable of constructive leadership; the functions it performs most effectively are those of criticism and investigation rather than responsibility for the direction of affairs. It is, indeed, true of any legislative assembly that its coherence for action depends upon its being so organized that it acts under a continuous sense of responsibility. This the Congress does not do, and, as I shall argue, from its own inherent nature can hardly do. And since the cabinet is no more than the president's advisory council, to be used in the degree, but no more than the degree, that he thinks fit, it cannot be looked to for initiative of this kind. The only person responsibly charged with thinking and planning in terms of the whole Union is the president; and it is a striking, even startling, feature of the American scheme of government that he has no way of seeing that his conception of his duty will, as a normal feature of the political process, be weighed from the angle that he considers imperative.

He has, of course, ways at his disposal of enforcing consideration. A message from the president, especially upon an important matter, is always news that will be nationally debated. The president can also, through the press and radio, insure that Congress is driven to take some action upon his proposals. And his patronage gives him a power of bringing pressure to bear upon individuals of both houses that is bound to count for a good deal. What he cannot assure to himself is that the policy he sets will be his policy. He must always take account of the fact that the Congress is a co-ordinate authority, jealous of its rights, likely, except in the gravest emergency, to resent any attempt upon his part to enforce his views upon its acceptance.

It is likely, indeed, to emphasize some divergence from those views in order to make it plain that he is not its master. This will be the case even when the party he leads is in power in both houses; his position will, naturally, be immensely more difficult when the opposition party controls one or both of the houses. Then, the whole interest of the opposition is to paralyze the presidential office in order to have the best possible chance of victory at the next election. How devastating that situation can be was decisively shown in the last two years of President Wilson's second administration.

It is, of course, an answer to this view to urge that its assumptions involve the idea of an executive responsible to the legislature in the British sense; and it is plain that this has been at no point a characteristic of the American scheme. But my argument is based upon a different foundation. It assumes only that the political evolution of the last forty years has shown that the modern state requires a strong executive, whose plans, of course suitably criticized and controlled, form the staple food of legislative digestion. I am arguing that the presidential conception of political needs must overwhelmingly square with the legislative conception if there is to be effective responsibility in government. The inference I draw from American experience is that this responsibility is minimized by the system. That was relatively unimportant before the Civil War; it has become increasingly important since that time. And though it is true that, on the whole, presidential leadership has been far more thoroughgoing since the Civil War than before it, that has been due, not to a public nor to a congressional recognition that it must be the case, but to external necessities that have imposed it. And, generally, both Congress and a good deal of public opinion, especially business opinion, have sought, at the earliest opportunity, to escape from the consequences of these essential necessities. The facts make against the continuous recognition of what is involved in leadership in the positive state. The risks a strong president must encounter if he wishes to exert his strength are both profound and manifold. He is not only running counter to the purpose of the Constitution. He is also arraying against himself all the forces in American politics to whom his strength is bound to be obnoxious. And included in those forces is Congress itself. For the greater his strength appears, the more he appears to dwarf Congress by its exercise. The more, accordingly, he tempts it to seek a trial of strength with him in order that it may vindicate its own claims to its co-ordinate share in power. The gravity of this position is obvious.

For the question it raises goes to the root of the whole scheme of American government. Just as it is an open question whether the division of powers between the federal government and the states is any longer compatible with efficient administration, even more, with full response to social needs,[8] so it is an open question whether the system of checks and bal-

[8] Cf. my article in the *New Republic* of May 3, 1939, "The Obsolescence of Federalism."

ances is not incompatible, as it is now operated, with a proper relation between executive and legislature. Even if we grant that the strong practical instinct of Americans has done much to lessen the creaking of the machine, the price that has to be paid for that diminution is a very heavy one. It is, no doubt, a price that a strong and courageous president will always be willing to pay; and it is no doubt true, also, that the stronger and more courageous he is the more likely he will be to enlist an effective public opinion on his side. But it is perhaps equally true that his strength and courage will seem to his critics to be more like blindness and obstinacy; and the measure of their exercise may serve to exacerbate opposition rather than to defeat it. Nor is there assurance that, when the time demands great leadership, it will be necessarily forthcoming. A good deal of the tragedy of the American depression might have been avoided if it were certain that the hour would produce the man. In fact, there is no such certainty. There is rather the danger that, in any save the gravest crisis, any continuous attempt to transcend the implications of the checks and balances will result in the charge of dictatorship. There is no charge to which, rightly enough, American public opinion is more sensitive, and there is none, therefore, that an American president is more anxious to avoid. But his very anxiety to avoid it means that he is continually searching for paths of compromise in realms where he doubts its wisdom.

The system, in fact, allows only a very great man to be himself. Even as strong a personality as Theodore

[23]

Roosevelt was broken by the system. Few presidents have avowed more frankly the price prudence exacts for the right to walk boldly along the highroad; and the record of Theodore Roosevelt is largely one of immense verbal emphasis and actual timidity. Indeed, despite his thunder and lightning, in his own favorite realm of "trust-busting," the record of President Taft, whom he accounted a weak president, is somewhat more impressive. It is unlikely that presidential courage will again encounter so bitter a fate as Andrew Johnson's. But Johnson's experience, with the vast repercussions it has had on American history, is important evidence of what the system of checks and balances can effect. It cannot only paralyze the presidential office. It may have the far more evil effect of completely destroying any idea of responsibility in government. And this dissipation of responsibility will matter far more in the coming years than it has done at any previous stage of American history, simply because the need of a positive policy will be greater. The problems that the United States will confront are, both in scale and complexity, far more delicate than those of any previous time.

It may be said that this is to exaggerate the position. The president, after all, may not be right; and the predominance of the cabinet over the House of Commons shows, it may be argued, the excessive penalties attached to executive control over the legislature. I am not here urging that a president is infallible; the evidence is too grimly the other way. My argument is, first, that a democracy needs clear direction, and that

[24]

it cannot get this unless the central motive force in a political system rests in the executive's hands. He may be right or wrong; what is important is that the plans put into operation should essentially be plans for which he is willing to accept full responsibility. And, secondly, it is not possible in the modern state to separate legislation from administration. In the making of policy, an assembly as miscellaneous as a legislature is bound to be cannot organize itself for creative action unless those who direct organization are also those who will apply it in action. In the United States, this is not the case. There is always a separation, which, at times, may amount to an antithesis, between them. The system, in fact, gives to the legislature functions which, nearly three-quarters of a century ago, John Stuart Mill pointed out it is least fitted to perform. As it is constructed, the interest of the legislature is to avoid the accusation of being a rubber stamp for presidential policy. To emphasize that avoidance, it always tends to develop a policy of its own. It is always inclined to build as much as possible upon the independence of its initiative in matters of legislation. This is bound to mean the erosion of responsibility. For the president can always claim that the policy by which he is bound is not his policy; while the legislature, in its turn, insists that the failure of a measure lies in the weakness of its application. Public opinion has rarely the materials upon which to form a valid judgment; and the matter involved, as in the realm of currency, for example, may be one upon which it is very difficult, from its nature, for any judgment to be formed at all.[9]

3

No one can examine the character of the American presidency without being impressed by its many-sidedness. The range of the president's functions is enormous. He is ceremonial head of the state. He is a vital source of legislative suggestion. He is the final source of all executive decision. He is the authoritative exponent of the nation's foreign policy. To combine all these with the continuous need to be at once the representative man of the nation and the leader of his political party is clearly a call upon the energies of a single man unsurpassed by the exigencies of any other political office in the world. In England, the main burden of ceremonial is taken from the shoulders of the prime minister by members of the royal family; and his political obligations are shared with a cabinet in which two or three other men are likely to carry a considerable part of his responsibility. The prime minister, moreover, knows that, in all normal circumstances, he will not have to face a recalcitrant House of Commons.

The ceremonial side of the presidency is, no doubt, fatiguing and delicate rather than important; but it is a great call upon the physical powers of any man. The president may on Monday be accepting a portrait of George V for the National Gallery at Washington.

[9] Cf. the debates in Congress on the proposed renewal of the president's power to devalue the dollar. *New York Times*, June 28-July 1, 1939.

He may have to greet the Daughters of the American Revolution on Tuesday, and the National Education Association on Wednesday. Washington's birthday calls for one kind of speech, and Jefferson's birthday, from a Democrat, for another. There may be a message to the Boy Scouts, a royal visitor from another country, the dinner to the judiciary (no easy matter when the president is at variance with the majority of the Supreme Court), the necessary entertainment of the diplomatic corps. He has to see enough of the Congress to make it feel that, at the least, it is not socially neglected. Attention must be paid to ceremonial recognition of the defense forces. A great government experiment, like Boulder Dam or Grand Coulee, must be visited. There must be tours at least wide enough in scope to give the impression that the president realizes that the United States is not merely Washington; and each of these must be chosen with an eye to its political repercussions. Any such tour, moreover, exacts an orgy of long speeches, the omission of any of which may offend an important district or a congressman whose support is significant. All of this, in its range and intensity, is enough to occupy the full attention of a single man. And all of this is conducted in a blare of pitiless publicity which makes the lightest word or act of the president, even of his wife,[10] a possible theme of national discussion.

But ceremony is, of course, merely the decorative penumbra of the office. It is the range of functions, and the pressure under which decisions have to be taken,

[10] Cf. William Allen White, *A Puritan in Babylon* (1938), pp. 353-7.

which, given their responsible character, constitute the immense burden of the office. And this burden will be the greater, the more positively the office is conceived. The president may get some aid (though less than one might expect) from his cabinet. He may get some more from those trusted advisers in non-official positions upon whom, it is probable, the modern president is coming more and more to rely. No doubt, too, the presence in Congress of a group of trusted politicians, of whose impact upon both houses he can be sure, counts for a good deal; it relieves the sense of an ever constant need for unrelaxing vigilance at the Capitol. But when all possible deductions have been made, there is no problem of which it cannot be said that it may be material upon which the president, and no one but the president, must make up his mind. Upon most of them he cannot hope to be an expert. Upon most of them, also, the people will look for some pronouncement from him; and upon most of those pronouncements he must expect the most expert criticism that opposition can produce. For it is by that criticism that the opposition hopes to replace him. Nothing that he can do is immune from public scrutiny; everything that he attempts may be the subject of the most rigorous investigation. He knows that, from the day he takes office, all that can be said against his policies legitimately, and, not seldom, illegitimately, is certain to be said.

What are the qualities called for by so vast and intense a range of functions? Above all, I think, the power to handle men, the ability almost intuitively to recognize the efficient human instrument for his purpose. That power has been more rare than is usually imagined. Lincoln, for instance, though he had an amazing insight into character, was never able to discover those instruments; no small part of the history of his administration is the record of his painful effort to transcend the results of that situation. Franklin Roosevelt has possessed it, as he showed when he chose, in remarkable circumstances, Mr. Ickes to be his secretary of the interior. Woodrow Wilson lacked it very largely; and no doubt a good deal of his final tragedy was due to that lack. So, also, did Calvin Coolidge; and he thereby prepared the road which led straight to the great depression.

There is the need for a president to come to office not only with a sense of the general direction in which he wishes to move, but with a sense, also, of the direction in which the times require him to move; these are very different things. Mr. Coolidge knew that he wished to pursue a policy of masterly inactivity; he assumed that the less he hampered the activities of business men the more prosperous would be the position of the country. The result of that attitude was an encouragement of speculative finance which he did not know enough to check at the right time, and which had assumed such proportions by the time Mr. Hoover took office that it is at least doubtful whether the latter would have been in a position to check it even if he had wished to do so.

And a president, further, must be able to think and decide rapidly; time is of the essence of perhaps half of his decisions. He needs not only the pertinacity to abide by them when they are made, but the instinct which tells him both when to give way and when he may wisely return to a policy about which he has been compelled at one stage to give way. Few things better illustrate this sense of time than President Wilson's approach to the problem of American intervention in the War of 1914. He created an atmosphere in which the mass of the people was persuaded to accept his view that intervention was inescapable; and he took, accordingly, a practically united people into the war. Had he acted much before he did, that psychological success would have been dubious enough at least to risk the chance of his re-election in 1916. The same quality is apparent in Franklin Roosevelt's handling of the neutrality issue. Again and again his search for the acceptance of his own formulae of international policy has been baffled by the dislike of the American people for European entanglements. Again and again, also, the president has utilized the changing circumstances to drive home the necessity of his view. If it be said that his problem has been rendered easier by the brutality of German and Italian policy since 1933, it has been rendered constantly more difficult by American doubt, which he may himself conceivably have shared, whether the governments of France and England read into his formulae the same ends as he sought to secure.

The presidential ability to co-ordinate is fundamental; and this largely depends upon the ability to distinguish between the significant and the insignificant.

The president who cannot delegate, and trust when he has delegated, is lost. For the most part, he can only concern himself with outlines; the details of the picture must be filled in by subordinates. Here, certainly, an art is required which must operate upon a scale quite different from any with which a prime minister is concerned. For the dignity of cabinet colleagues, and the relative certainty with which he can control the House of Commons, means that he is free, once policy in the large is settled, to leave its implementation alone. But a president may lose a bill in Congress if a subordinate proceeds untactfully. His strategy of action is necessarily far more delicate than any English prime minister requires. Every delegation of power is therefore a risk to be taken, and this makes his judgment of men a matter of supreme importance. He must know that the men he uses will see things through his eyes. He must feel confident not only that they will not bother him unduly, but even more that they will refer back to him at the point where his pressure only can produce the required result. He must delegate, too, knowing that at best he is bound to make mistakes both in men and in things. This is above all the case in matters of foreign policy. There, he is dependent upon the eyes and ears of men who, however skilfully he chooses them, will be less under his control and influence in Paris or London than in Washington. And the men to whom he delegates complicate his problem because they must delegate in their turn. Anyone who considers the relation of Lincoln to Stanton will see that the issue is an intricate one. To go too far is to risk the fulfilment of his aims; not to go far enough is to overwhelm himself in a multiplicity of detail which may no less jeopardize those aims.

Any president, almost in the nature of things, is in a position of aloofness. The eminence of his position is so great, the calls upon him so numerous, that it is not easy for him to avoid a sense of profound separation from his fellows. He cannot cultivate the kind of intimacy with his critics that is born of the almost instinctive good-fellowship of the House of Commons. He is rarely dealing, either in his cabinet or in his party-relations, with men to whose intimate friendship he has become accustomed by long experience. It is difficult for him to build a body of friends outside his official family upon whom he can rely for advice and action; the experience of Mr. Wilson with Colonel House, and of Franklin Roosevelt with Mr. Moley, shows that this is the case. In the result, a president who is to do his job adequately requires certain psychological qualities which cannot be too sufficiently emphasized. He must not be an unduly sensitive person. By his position, he is the central target for criticism, and he must be able to shake off its effect without repining. The danger of an inability to immunize himself against attack is shown clearly by Mr. Wilson's career in the White House. A president, no doubt, needs self-confidence; but he must not have that arrogant self-confidence which assumes, first, that his policies are infallibly right, and, therefrom, that criticism of them is original sin. It is pretty evident, from the documents, that Mr. Wilson lacked this ability to withstand attack. When he was pricked he bled, and he magnified the authors of the pinpricks into assassins. The result was that he predominantly surrounded himself, as in his cabinet, with second-rate men whom he could always overbear by superior intelligence, or, outside it, with men like Colonel House who were prepared simply to indulge in agreement for the pleasurable sensation of living at the center of power. At every critical moment after 1917, therefore, Mr. Wilson never had the personal instruments upon whom he could depend. He had either enemies whom he could not trust, or friends who had been sterilized into ineffective silence. A president in that position is bound to risk, and probably meet, disaster.

I do not mean that a president must not possess self-confidence; he could not do his work without a considerable measure of it. He has to pass judgment upon a mass of problems, not least in international affairs, upon which his actual knowledge must be small. Unless he was able to feel reliance upon that judgment, clearly he would fall into the hands of any associate strong-minded enough to establish an ascendency over him. Broadly, indeed, it is true to say that a lack of self-confidence has not been the besetting sin of presidents; Buchanan apart, it is difficult to think of one in whom irresolution was the outstanding characteristic. In general, it is almost true to say that entrance upon the office itself breeds self-confidence; that is interestingly true in the case of men so different as Polk and Coolidge. The problem for the president is to have sufficient of it to be able to plow ahead in his own way, and yet never so much that he is insensitive to the significance of counsel and criticism. He will get both in abundance, and the delicacy of his task, as Lincoln so supremely knew, lies above all in being able to make himself sufficiently remote from both as to be certain that it is his own mind that is making the decision.

I have spoken of the aloofness which surrounds the presidential office. No one can watch the president at work without the sense of its profundity, and the realization, therefore, that in an ultimate way, the president is bound to be a lonely man. I do not mean lonely in the sense that Lincoln was lonely; Lincoln's loneliness derived from an inner and utter melancholy that gave him friends but never intimates. His ultimate self was always withdrawn from his fellows; the greater the responsibility he bore, the greater was his loneliness. It is clear, for instance, that his famous story-telling was, above all, a protective coloration against its consequences upon his relations. I mean a loneliness that comes partly from the knowledge that no one can share the steep eminence upon which he is poised, and that, therefore, no one can really share the burden of responsibility he has to carry.

This fact, I think, makes two things important. No president must be too far ahead of his time if he is to be a successful president. He must see what he sees with the eyes of the multitude upon whose shoulders he stands. To get anywhere he must win understanding; to win it, the policy he pursues must never be so remote from the views about him that he cannot get that understanding. At bottom, his real power is in the popular support he can rally for the direction he proposes to follow; and it is generally unlikely that he will be able to rally support of any considerable volume for the novel plan or the unlooked-for principle. A good illustration of this was, I think, the Court plan of President Roosevelt in 1937. There, it is interesting to note, while he sought an objective intelligible to, and sympathized with, by that great majority which renewed his power in 1936, he sought its achievement by ways with which the tradition had not familiarized the masses; in ways, indeed, to which the tradition had made the masses hostile. He was too ingenious, both in concept and in mechanism, for a multitude which sees the broad highways only. He had insufficiently prepared it for so circuitous a divagation from those highways. It is the one instance, so far, in Mr. Roosevelt's presidency in which his hold of the opinion upon which presidential power depends was unsure in method and defective in execution. The result was his resounding defeat. I suspect that when the secret history of the Court proposals comes to be written we shall find that no small part of that defeat was the outcome of lesser men's urgency prevailing over his own normal realization that the way to win the confidence of the people is to take them fully into your confidence. On the Court fight, he was not in a realm made familiar to him by technical experts; and he made the mistake of relying upon advisers who did not understand that no statesman can ever successfully attack fundamental institutions by sidestepping them.

The president must never be ahead of his time; he achieves the maximum unity by moving to objectives that are expected as well as desired. And, in so moving, it is important that he should always retain the common touch without ever being controlled by it. A president who lacks this gift, the two Adamses, for example, is bound to suffer defeat. Without this gift, the presidential power to rally opinion in his support is paralyzed. Andrew Jackson always gave his forces the impression that his thoughts were theirs; he symbolized them in a way that made them an army of adherents. Lincoln marvelously made the ordinary man feel that the tragic sufferings of the war were his sufferings too. Mr. Roosevelt's use of the radio has made him a living and intimate part of millions of homes in which, otherwise, his policies would have been remote abstractions. He has symbolized to them, in an epoch of economic crisis, that zeal for the "forgotten man" which millions have wished to see embodied in the contours of policy. It is this absence of the common touch that was, I think, largely responsible for the defeat of Mr. Hoover. He was full of good will; he worked relentlessly at his task. But he never gave his constituents the impression of entering into their problems upon the plane on which they encountered them. He saw them from angles so different that, so to say, they did not seem the same problems. And since the remedies he recommended were those which, in the previous two years, the electorate had been engaged in largely repudiating, the general impression was conveyed (though quite wrongly conveyed) that Mr. Hoover simply did not realize there was a crisis at all.

What I am seeking to argue was well put by Bagehot in a classic discussion of Sir Robert Peel. A democratic statesman, he said, must be "an uncommon man of common opinions." That, I think, is as good a description as any of the successful president. The nature of the office requires a man who is marching with his times and is not remote from them. The things he must emphasize in his policy, however ingeniously he elaborates them, must be the big themes of common discussion. Vast innovations for which the public is unprepared are almost bound to fail, because they are almost certain to shock. There can be experiment in the tactics of policy; there can hardly, without great danger, be experiment in fundamental ideas. Those observers who say that Mr. Roosevelt missed a great opportunity in 1933 when he did not nationalize the banking system seem to me wholly to misconceive the nature of the presidential office. While it is possible that, at that grave moment, the president might have carried through such a scheme, it was so widely outside the range of common expectation that it would have destroyed his authority for the rest of his term of office. Nothing in previous discussion had prepared the public for such a measure. Nothing in the electoral conception of Mr. Roosevelt had prepared the public to associate him with such a strategy. He might have won the battle; he would have lost the campaign. For in democratic politics, the justification for drastic expedients is long familiarity with the idea; their possible coming must be part of the current coin of political controversy. Otherwise, the routine of the common man is dangerously disturbed; and once that occurs, he easily becomes the victim of those manufactured panics which are the staple opportunities of men like Hitler or Huey Long.

He must have "common opinions." But it is equally imperative that he be an "uncommon man." The public must see themselves in him, but they must, at the same time, be confident that he is something bigger than themselves. They must see someone who compels respect. They must see someone who can say in the grand way what they half-articulately feel. They must have the sense that they are a part of significant events. Dull government can only endure when government is unimportant; a long period of extraordinary prosperity will, as in the Coolidge regime, persuade men that dullness is the same as soundness. But where any significant part of the population is hard pressed, it looks to the president for relief; and it is then urgent that he give the appearance of active intervention on their behalf. A dull president will not last long in a period of crisis. His temptation, just because he is dull, is to throw the burden of responsibility upon the leaders in Congress. He thus ceases to be the symbol of action, and the nation feels deprived of that leadership to which it feels itself entitled. It was a sound instinct which persuaded Theodore Roosevelt, when he was in the White House, always to provide a public pronouncement for Monday morning. It was a still more sound instinct which led Woodrow Wilson to revive the custom, which had lapsed since Jefferson's time, of addressing Congress in person. And it has, I think, been something like a stroke of genius on the part of Franklin Roosevelt to transform the press conference at the White House from the stiff interchange that took place under his predecessors to the full and frank discussions of which we have now so intimate and revealing a record.[11] To make the public see how some, at least, of the wheels go round is to admit them to a sense of the range and magnitude of the office. That is one of the ways in which a masterful president can do most to educate his electorate to the understanding of his policies. It is, of course, part of the technique of propaganda, as well as of information, and, as such, has its very real dangers.[12] The president may say the wrong thing,[13] or he may be misrepresented; and there is the danger of premature disclosure. But, all in all, the White House press conference is probably a necessary method of driving home to an electorate of nearly fifty millions the presidential attitude of mind. It cannot compete with a good radio address as a source of direct impact; but the latter is a weapon likely to diminish in value if it makes the president oppressively familiar. There is an important sense in which his remoteness is not less important than his friendliness as an instrument in making effective his policy.

There is no formula for the "uncommon man"; his

[11] See *The Public Papers and Addresses of Franklin D. Roosevelt*, Vols. I-V, for a full sample of them.
[12] Lindsay Rogers, *The American Senate* (1926), pp. 215 f.
[13] For an amusing example see Rogers, *op. cit.*, p. 218.

qualities vary with the person who fills the office. It is one thing with Washington, and a very different thing with Jefferson or Madison. It is one thing with Andrew Jackson, and again, a very different thing with Franklin Roosevelt. In general, it is worth noting that, even with ordinary men, the momentum of the office has the power to call out the best that is in them. James Polk had few exceptional qualities either of mind or of character; yet it is difficult to read his *Diary* without the sense that he grew consistently in stature throughout his incumbency in the White House. There was nothing intellectually extraordinary in Grover Cleveland; yet his rugged obstinacy gave his periods of office a certain distinction which has had its influence upon the subsequent tradition of the presidency. Colorless presidents, indeed, have been more exceptional than the critics have been wont to admit; Franklin Pierce, Fillmore, James Buchanan, Benjamin Harrison, and Warren Harding stand out in this regard. The fact is that the opportunities the office affords are so great that an ordinary man is usually dignified by it, while an exceptional man is stimulated as by no other post in a democratic state. Partly, I think, this arises from its very elevation. The depth of interest it evokes among the American people is a challenge to the best in a man. Bagehot, with his usual prescience, has noted the extraordinary growth in Lincoln's stature during his presidency. That is, of course, outstanding, though perhaps less remarkable in so great a figure than in the case of lesser men from whom, on the previous evidence, so much less was to be expected.

The cases of Tyler and Polk are more outstanding; for without the office neither would have seemed, historically, the exceptional man he became. The influence of the office on the personality of its holder is, in fact, a fascinating study in the dynamics of political power.

4

The founders of the Constitution were especially proud of the method they adopted for choosing the president; none of their expectations has been more decisively disappointed. The presidential candidates are now chosen at national conventions of the respective parties; and the decision is made by the whole electorate, voting in such fashion that, as shown in several elections, a plurality of votes does not necessarily carry with it the certainty of election. It is, indeed, a desirable thing that the method should be made to correspond to the facts. A constitutional amendment which simply stated that the candidate with the most votes should be deemed to have been elected would be a wise safeguard against possible difficulties in the future.

An American presidential convention is like nothing else in the civilized world; and the critics of the system—which, in its modern form, is just a hundred years old—have exhausted the language of vituperation in attack upon its character. The power of money; the persuasive power of hidden and corrupt influence; the undue authority of the "doubtful" state; the overt and hidden prejudices against particular types of candidates, as, for instance, members of the Roman Catholic Church; the "deals" which accompany the capture of a delegation for one candidate as against another; the mythology of the "favorite son"; the casual influence, notable in the case of Lincoln's selection, of the choice of the convention city; the undue impact, as in the Democratic convention of 1896, of a single speech by a potential nominee; the operation of the technique of the "dark horse" candidate; the exploitation of the "stalking-horse" behind whom some well-organized group has its carefully prepared selection whose name is put forward at the right moment; and, finally, the raucous, complex, and hectic atmosphere of the convention itself; its well-improvised enthusiasms; its fantastic horse-play; its immunity to thought; its wild rumors; its incredible conspiracies; all these characteristics, none of which can ever suffer exaggeration, seem to the outsider, and especially to the European outsider, about the worst possible way in which to choose a man to occupy the highest executive post in a democratic commonwealth.

The convention itself is, of course, predominantly an organ for registering decisions that have been made behind the scenes. Occasionally, an utterance upon its floor may exercise a real influence upon its outcome. Senator Conkling did Grant irreparable damage in 1880; and the contrast between his speech and that of Garfield, who nominated Sherman, had a good deal to do with the emergence of Garfield as the Republican candidate. So, also, the famous speech of Bryan in 1896 turned the balance of opinion in his favor. But in general the actual nomination is decided in part by the pre-convention campaign and in part by bargains actually concluded in and around the convention itself. The pre-convention campaign is of great importance. It was decisive, for instance, in the selection of Franklin Roosevelt in 1932; the spadework done by Mr. Farley in the two preceding years was the condition precedent to his nomination. Bargaining at the convention is, of course, a special art. Its importance emerges either when there are a number of outstanding candidates between whom choice is difficult—as with the Republicans in 1880 and 1920, and with the Democrats in 1924—or when a powerful group has made up its mind to try to force a "dark horse" upon the convention. Accident, in fact, plays a much smaller part in the choice of the candidate than is imagined. Many people, for example, expected either Governor Lowden or General Wood to be the Republican candidate in 1920; and immense sums had been expended in promoting their interests. But the skilful proponents of Senator Harding's name had long foreseen that the acuteness of their rivalry would make neither possible, and they had long foreseen the probability of Harding's success. "At the proper time after the Republican national convention meets," said Mr. Daugherty, Senator Harding's manager, "some fifteen men, bleary-eyed with loss of sleep, and perspiring profusely with the excessive heat, will sit down in seclusion round a big table. I will be with them, and will present the [name] of Senator Harding to them and before we get through, they will put him over."[14] That is precisely what occurred.

Out of all this complexity, there has emerged the doctrine of "availability." The party needs a candidate who, positively, will make the widest appeal and, negatively, will offend the least proportion of the electorate. On the whole, he ought to come from a doubtful state; a Democrat from New York is more "available" than one from the solid South because he is likely to win votes which might otherwise be uninterested. It seems still to be true that it is difficult to elect a Roman Catholic; half the solid South refused to vote for Governor Smith in 1928. He must not be anti-religious; that would offend the great vested interest of the churches. He must be sound on the tariff; he must be against wild currency adventures; he must not be too overtly internationalist in outlook. Administrative experience, like the governorship of a state, is important. It is helpful if he is a self-made man; the "log cabin to White House" tradition is still, despite the two Roosevelts, an influential one. He ought not to possess any nostrum which can be represented as extreme. In the aftermath of a war period, it is important that he should have played his part in the army; from Jackson and Taylor onwards, the military hero has had an immense appeal to the electorate. It is undesirable that he should have too close an association with the big interests, especially Wall Street; Wilson, in 1912, owed his

[14] *New York Times*, June 13, 1920. For a full account of Mr. Daugherty's technique, see H. M. Daugherty and Thomas Dixon, *The Inside Story of the Harding Tragedy* (1932), pp. 32-55.

[44]

nomination to Mr. Bryan's famous pronouncement that he would not support anyone under obligation to "Morgan, Ryan, Belmont, or any other member of the privilege-seeking favor-hunting class." He must have a sufficiently flexible mind to accept the implications of the trading necessary to build his majority. He must not be the kind of man whom it is obviously easy to ridicule in a campaign, either because he is "viewy," or for any other reason.

All of which means, as a general rule, that the outcome of a presidential convention is likely to be a compromise of some kind. But it is important to realize that it is not a compromise in which, without cause, the outstanding candidate is certain to be defeated. Henry Clay never became president because the political judgment of his party warned it against nominating him in the years when its chances for success were brightest. Blaine never became president because even many of his admirers profoundly felt that his association, to say no more, with dubious political methods left too much to be explained away. Governor Fuller of Massachusetts could not be nominated because, as Senator Borah said, Sacco and Vanzetti would thereby have become issues in the campaign.[15] Senator Lodge was for forty years an outstanding figure in the Senate. But he could not have secured the Republican nomination simply because his own party realized that, whatever his qualities, those years in politics were a continuous demonstration of his unfitness for high

[15] As governor of his state in 1927, Mr. Fuller did not intervene to prevent their execution.

executive office. Mr. Hoover was undoubtedly the leading Republican in 1936; and, on the precedent of Cleveland's nomination in 1892, was the natural recipient of the candidature. But he was unavailable because the party leaders felt, quite rightly, that he was too closely associated with Republican failure in the depression to be an acceptable candidate.

It is notable, in short, that whenever an obvious contender for the nomination does not receive it, there is usually a quite adequate explanation for his failure. It is notable, further, that when a "dark horse" nominee emerges, he has been held in reserve for just such an opportunity by powerful influences which are waiting for their moment. It is possible for someone, like Franklin Pierce, who is unknown to the general public, to emerge from the ordeal. But it is to be noticed that, if he does, his emergence is always due to special circumstances, and that there is to be detected behind him a substantial cohort who know precisely what they are doing. A "dark horse," that is to say, is a compromise candidate in much the same way as Mr. Bonar Law was a compromise between Sir Austen Chamberlain and Mr. Walter Long in 1911, or Sir Henry Campbell-Bannerman as Liberal leader after 1895. Much the same situation obtains in the complicated intrigues of French politics. It is difficult for the outsider to follow the tortuous internal events which make now M. Herriot, now M. Chautemps, and now M. Daladier the leader of the Socialist Radicals. Immediacy on the basis of "availability" there also explains the result that is reached. It is as natural for

Henry Clay or James G. Blaine to have missed the presidency as it is for Lord Curzon or Sir Austen Chamberlain to have missed the premiership in their country.

The real difference, of course, lies in the prior experience of those who are chosen as nominees. Other things being equal, a prime minister in Great Britain or France will have served a long apprenticeship in the legislative assembly before obtaining the supreme office. He will be a figure in the House. He will be known to the party. He will probably have had considerable administrative experience in a lesser office. He will be pretty intimately known to those whom he is to lead. In the United States, none of this is necessarily true. Since the Civil War, a distinguished career in Congress has rarely been a passport to the nomination. Attainment of cabinet office has had no direct relevance to a candidature in any except two cases; and, of these, Mr. Hoover's name was made rather by his war record than by his experience in the Department of Commerce. A state governorship has counted for much. But it is pretty true to say that most of the chosen candidates have been names in the nation rather than in Washington. They have not known with any intimacy those with whom they would, as president, be expected to work.

The position is in curious contrast with the pre-Civil War period. The first four presidents of the United States almost nominated themselves; and, among their successors, there was hardly a candidate for the nomination who was not a person of considerable political consequence. One feature, indeed, is constant. No presidential candidate in the whole record has been a business man. The vocation, clearly, is a full-time one; and the qualities which make for business success make, also, against the possibility of nomination. It is true that, in his engineering period, Mr. Hoover was mainly a company organizer. But after his return to America all his energies were devoted to politics. Business men have played a not inconsiderable part in the conventions as king-makers; but it is a curious fact that in a civilization perhaps more dominated by business men than by any other, they have had to surrender the hope of being king. The lawyer, the soldier, the rentier and politician, the man who lives by his earnings as politician; these are the types from whom the candidates have been chosen. The business man may hope for cabinet office. He is likely to be important in negativing ambitions the realization of which would not be regarded with favor by the big interests. But, on the record, he must be the power behind the throne; he cannot hope to occupy it.

The reason, I think, is simple. The small man cannot hope to afford the risks of a political career. The great one, a Rockefeller, a Vanderbilt, even an Owen D. Young, would not be an "available" candidate simply because he would arouse the suspicion that the party which nominated him was in bondage to the money-power. The influence of the business outlook upon the parties must, therefore, be indirect. It is real enough, as the election of McKinley makes clear. But it must always seek to veil itself in a decent obscur-

ity if it is not to prove a source of violent opposition
from the interests of labor and the small farmer.
Franklin Roosevelt gained great strength from both
these sources by the fact that the Liberty League, an
organization dominated by the great business interests,
was opposed to his re-election.

The big problem that is raised by the American
method of nominating presidential candidates is
whether it puts a premium, as Lord Bryce argued,
against the opportunity of first-rate men to receive
consideration. I do not think his case is proved by
making a list of first-rate men, Clay and Calhoun and
Webster, for example, who missed nomination. The
answer to that argument is, first, that many first-rate
men have become president by reason of the system;
and second, that the reasons which stopped others
would have been powerful reasons against their elevation in any representative democracy. It is, I think,
at least doubtful whether the elevation of a Roman
Catholic to the premiership would be regarded favor-
ably in Great Britain. A great business man, both in
England and France, will operate mainly behind the
political scene rather than in front of it; of our three
business men who have become prime ministers one
was, in fact, a rentier, and the others had long retired
from active participation therein. Few people could
easily explain the nuances that account for the failure
of one man to reach the top, and the success of another. And in estimating the meaning of "availability" we must remember, always, that there is a real
sense in which the more strong the candidate, suppos-

ing that he represents a special point of view, the more strong, also, are likely to be his enemies. Not infrequently, an easy nomination—so long as the renomination of an existing president is not involved—merely means, as it meant with Horace Greeley in 1872, with Judge Parker in 1904, with Governor Landon in 1936, that rival candidates do not consider there is much prospect for their party's success, and they are not anxious to be associated with a dismal failure at the polls, with a view of a later nomination.

Granted, this is to say, the greatness of the prize, and the necessity of popular election, it is difficult to see what other method than the nominating convention is available; more, it is true to say that, on balance, it has worked well rather than badly. The criticisms that are brought against it are rather, in their real substance, criticisms of the place of the presidency in the American constitutional scheme than of the method whereby the president is chosen. It is regrettable that an inexperienced man may come to reside in the White House; the answer is that few of those who have reached it have been inexperienced men. If it be said that men like Harding and Coolidge were unfit for the great post they secured, the answer is that the first had considerable experience both in the Ohio legislature and in the Senate, while the second had been a successful Massachusetts politician, twice occupying the governorship, for twenty years. If we take the presidents of the twentieth century, there is not one who had not been prepared for presidential office by a long experience of politics; and, with the possible exception of the Democratic candidate in 1904, that is true, also, of their defeated rivals. What is lacking in their training is mostly the art of handling Congress; and the rules of that art are only partly dependent upon the character of the president for the time.

It must be remembered that, in making the choice, there are two fundamental considerations in the background of which the meaning of "availability" must be set. The first is that the party choosing a candidate wants, if it can, to win; and second, it knows that if it does win, and its nominee becomes president, there is great likelihood of its having to adopt him a second time, since not to do so is to condemn an administration for which it has to bear responsibility. While, therefore, it is quite true that a party convention provides an opportunity for the art of such a dubious wire-puller as Mr. Daugherty, it is also true that the managers of a great party are anxious to avoid, if they can, the consequences of success in that type of manipulation. One has only to read the account of an experience of conventions like that of Senator Hoar of Massachusetts to see that a scrupulous and honorable man will approach the task of selection with all the seriousness that its consequences require.[16]

All in all, I doubt whether the methods of the system are very different from those of other countries. They are, perhaps, more open and crude than in Great Britain. There is no generosity in the fight for power. There is a passionate determination on the part

[16] G. F. Hoar, *Autobiography* (1903), I, 378-421.

of organized interests to get the "safe" man who can be relied upon to live up to the commitments exacted from him. There is the fierce conflict of rival ambitions. There is the organization of every sort of cabal to win a victory for its man. Press and radio and platform are vigorously manipulated to this end. Immense promises are made, pretty ugly deals are effected. Yet I suggest that anyone who knows the life of a political party from within Great Britain will not feel inclined to cast a stone at the American system. It fits, well enough, the medium in which it has to work. It achieves the results that the needs of the people require.

For there is at least one test of the system that is, I think, decisive. There have been five considerable crises in American history. There was the need to start the new republic adequately in 1789; it gave the American people its natural leader in George Washington. The crisis of 1800 brought Jefferson to the presidency; that of 1861 brought Abraham Lincoln. The War of 1914 found Woodrow Wilson in office; the great depression resulted in the election of Franklin Roosevelt. So far, it is clear, the hour has brought forth the man. It is of course true, as Bagehot said, that "success in a lottery is no argument for lotteries." I agree that no nation can afford a succession of what Theodore Roosevelt termed "Buchanan Presidents"— men whose handling of the issues is uncertain and feeble. But the answer is that the nation has never had that succession; an epoch of Hardings and Coolidges produces, by the scale of the problems to which

it gives rise, its own regeneration. The weak president, as I have argued, comes from the fact that a
strong predecessor has set the feet of the nation on
level ground. He is chosen because, after a diet of
strong occasions, a nation, like an individual, turns
naturally to the chance of a quiet time. "Normalcy"
is always certain to be popular after crises. The issue
is whether, when a crisis comes, the system can discover the man to handle it. On the evidence, this
has so far been very remarkably the case. To urge that
it is chance is, I think, a superficial view. It is the outcome of the national recognition that energy and
direction are required, and the man chosen is the
party response to that recognition. The phenomenon
is as natural as the replacement of Mr. Asquith by
Mr. Lloyd George in 1917, as instinctive, one may
say, as the widespread demand, in the England of
1939, for the strengthening of the personnel of the
"National" government. The American scheme involves delay; Mr. Roosevelt did not come to office
until the nation had suffered three years of depression.
But the essential fact is that he came to office. Nor is
there reason to suppose that this is accidental. The
more deeply we penetrate the working of the system
the more clearly does it emerge that the result is inherent in its nature.

5

Quite different considerations apply to the position
of a president after election. The tasks that confront
him even before he assumes the burden of office are

manifold. He has to choose, not merely his cabinet colleagues, but a vast horde of minor officials in an atmosphere that is not seldom akin to pandemonium. He has to work out at any rate some of the general principles of the policy he proposes to follow. He has to arrive at a *modus vivendi* with the leaders of his party in Congress. There are the delicate problems of the transition between the old regime and the new; two months now elapse between election and assumption of office. Every action of his, every thought almost, is surrounded by a fierce light of publicity which makes the calm appropriate to thought almost impossible. The historians have described the almost fantastic atmosphere which preceded the inauguration of Garfield, and ended in his assassination at the hands of a disappointed office seeker. More delicate even was the type of problem confronted by Franklin Roosevelt before his entrance into the White House on March 4, 1933. For President Hoover was still in office, even though discredited by defeat. The country was in a state of crisis; and Mr. Hoover was engaged in difficult negotiations about the international economic situation. On both aspects of policy, his views and those of Mr. Roosevelt were as far apart as the poles. He could hardly act without consulting his successful opponent; yet he was not prepared to act upon the only assumptions Mr. Roosevelt was prepared to accept. The complicated minuet they jointly performed in those months, with Mr. Hoover seeking collaboration on his own terms and Mr. Roosevelt delicately insisting that the responsibility was necessarily the president's, indicates the range of the issues the president-elect has to decide.

And he does not approach those issues as, in any full sense, a free man. The president is the subject of compulsions which begin to operate from the day he has been nominated as a candidate. He has to pay a price in men; he has to pay a price in measures. He has to reward the more outstanding, at least, of those who have been responsible for his election; how great that price may be will be evident to anyone who looks at the membership of President Harding's cabinet. To assure his election, he will have made or have acquiesced in the making of innumerable, and not seldom dubious, commitments. He will have had to placate or persuade vested interests, like Wall Street, or the farming community, or organized labor, or the Catholic vote. Some deference he must pay to the outline of the party platform; though here a convenient and rhetorical vagueness will usually leave him a diversity of possible interpretation. He has to think in terms of the profound sectionalism by which he is confronted. He has to bend his mind to decision upon a multiplicity of issues about which he has hardly before had to concern himself. It is not, I think, exaggeration to say that the day of a successful election is the day on which the president ceases to be a free man.

For there is not only the price, in men and measures, of election. There is the price for laying the foundations of a possible re-election; and that will begin almost as soon as he assumes the reins of office.

Few presidents have been willing to forgo the chance of a second term; and no president can so act as to deprive his party at least of the chance of a second term for its nominee. He has to pay the price exacted for the power to maintain the control of his party, above all in Congress; and there he is bound to remember that he faces a power which is, at best, coordinate with himself and may, unless skilfully handled, insist on seeking to become his superior rival. No doubt he can always appeal against it—as both Woodrow Wilson and Franklin Roosevelt have remarkably done—to the force of public opinion outside. But he can never be the master of his party in the sense that a British prime minister with a majority in the House of Commons is. He cannot appeal from an antagonistic Congress to an electorate whose support he believes himself to possess. He must persuade and cajole; he can rarely afford to threaten. Whatever be the growth in the magnitude of the executive power in the United States, in the nature of things it cannot even remotely be described, at least with accuracy, as approaching dictatorial proportions.

For the punitive powers by which a president can hew his way to his goal are cribbed and confined by the system at every turn. He can do something with the patronage; though the limits of its influence are, in the realm of major policy, more narrow than the critics of the executive are prone to admit. He cannot threaten a dissolution. He cannot even, as Franklin Roosevelt learned in the congressional elections of 1938, successfully appeal to his supporters to purge

the critics of his own party. His real reliance is simply upon the public opinion he can muster in his behalf. Two-thirds of the senators are largely beyond
his power of control; they were there before he came
to office, and they can normally expect to remain
there long after he has gone. And even though the
turnover of members of the House of Representatives is much greater than in the Senate, its proportions depend much more upon local than upon
national considerations, at least within the party itself. The experience of Franklin Roosevelt is, again,
decisive in this regard. The defeat of his plan for the
reform of the Supreme Court was, after all, accom-
plished by his opponents within six months of the
most triumphant victory in the history of the presidency.

Nor does presidential power have the right to confidence even when its majority in Congress is assured.
Behind and above its authority, there looms the Supreme Court which may, at any moment, strike an
act of Congress into impotence. And it cannot be
said that this depends merely upon the composition
of the Court, that a liberal president is safe if he
has a liberal majority there, and vice versa. In the
Schechter case,[17] all the liberal members of the Court
were united with their conservative colleagues to find
the National Industrial Recovery Act—one of the
most important, if one of the most dubious, experiments of Franklin Roosevelt's first term—unconstitutional. No president can seriously hope for a

[17] *Schechter* v. U. S. (1935), 295 U. S. 495.

constitutional amendment in this realm that is likely to be of assistance to him within the time-limit during which he must work. He may be fortunate in obtaining vacancies on the Court which he can fill with men of his own outlook; but he is bound to remember the experience of Theodore Roosevelt with Mr. Justice Holmes and know that not even the most careful scrutiny will give him a positive assurance that he will be upheld.[18] Here the truth is that the constitutional limits within which both the president and a Court that is scrupulous in its technique of interpretation must work are probably more narrow than the needs of the United States. On any showing, the powers left to the states cover matters which hamper the prospect of rapid and decisive federal action, should any number of them be recalcitrant; and the difficulties of the commerce clause, in the age of giant industry, will be obvious on the most superficial examination.[19]

No doubt in an emergency, the Supreme Court will act with a certain generosity or acumen; its attitude to the Adamson law in 1916[20] and to the gold clause in 1934[21] is proof that it is far from indifferent to the political consequences of its decisions. Members of the Supreme Court dwell upon Olympian heights; but they display all the human characteristics we associate

[18] *Correspondence between Theodore Roosevelt and H. C. Lodge* (1928), I, 517-519.

[19] Cf. E. S. Corwin, *The Twilight of the Supreme Court* (1936).

[20] *Wilson* v. *New* (1917), 243 U. S. 332.

[21] Cf. the interesting discussion of P. J. Eder. "The Gold Clause Cases in the Light of History," 23, Georgetown *Law Review*, pp. 359-388, 722-760.

with dwellers upon Olympus. Some of them, at least, are keen politicians by training, keen enough to yearn for the presidency even after they have become justices of the Supreme Court; it is not, indeed, an exaggeration to say that, at any given time, one or two of the justices are potential candidates for the presidency. It is not unimportant, in this context, that Chief Justice Taft did not think it incompatible with his high office to act as a personal adviser to Mr. Coolidge throughout his presidential terms;[22] and though we do not yet fully know the part played by Chief Justice Hughes and by some, at least, of his associates in the defeat of Mr. Roosevelt's Court plan in 1937, there can be little doubt that it was considerable. Any president who chooses to embark upon an ample legislative program, especially if it touches, as an ample program can hardly fail to touch, the delicate problems of the limits of the federal power, must keep one eye firmly fixed upon its possible repercussions upon the Supreme Court.

Not only is this the case upon any narrow partisan ground. Two, at least, of the great conflicts between the executive and the judiciary in American history rest upon a far wider foundation than that of narrow party advantage. That is certainly the case in the conflict between Marshall and Jefferson; it is also true of the conflict between Marshall and Jackson. In each instance, what was at stake was a philosophy of the Constitution. In each instance, also, it is easy to

[22] W. Allen White, *A Puritan in Babylon* (1938), pp. 245, 252, 284-288, 348-350, 374-376.

understand the wide differences which separated the protagonists. They were not at variance over a small measure. They were at variance over the pivotal question of the place of the judiciary in the American constitutional scheme. For Marshall, rightly or wrongly—I myself think wrongly—the duty of the Court was not merely to strengthen the national power; even more it was to strengthen it as a weapon of property against the possible assault of the masses. The whole ethos of his conception of the Court's function lay in his belief that the power of democracy must be limited by the right of property to security; and he saw in the instrument of judicial review the highroad to this end. Neither Jefferson nor Jackson sympathized with this outlook, and the issue was bound to be joined between them. It is bound, I add, to be joined—emergency apart—between the Court and any president who seeks a rapid redefinition of the place of property in the state. For to redefine that place means legislation which is, in its nature, not only bound to traverse basic precedents in the history of the Court; it runs very quickly toward a re-assessment of the division of powers contemplated by the Constitution. And since it is likely that, save in the most exceptional periods, the majority of the judges of the Court will be successful lawyers whose outlook has been shaped by long years of service to the business interests, they are not apt to view with favor legislation which seeks the control of these in a way likely to be regarded by business itself as detrimental to the national well-being.

A president, therefore, especially an actively liberal president, is bound to have regard to the possible attitude of the Court to his innovations; and he is bound to remember that only emergency will persuade the Court to abdicate from its historic function—the real achievement of Marshall—of guardian of the rights of property. But the compulsions upon him do not end there. He must pay continuous attention to the attitude of business itself. To disturb its confidence is, always, to jeopardize his chance of a smooth passage during his years of office. It is not merely that investment may lag, with its rapid repercussion upon unemployment and the standard of life. It is not merely, either, that American business is as powerful a "lobby" in Washington as there is anywhere in the world. It is also that the interstitial connections between business and politics in the United States give to its actions a quite special and immediate authority of which he dare not be neglectful. It is to big business that his party must look for essential campaign contributions. There are states whose senators depend upon some great corporation for their place in Washington. Its influence in the national committee of his party will always be profound. It will tend to have behind its views the main weight of the legal profession—a serious matter in a legislative system where the lawyer plays so large a part. The president who arouses the suspicion that he is not a "sound" man from the angle of business philosophy is bound to run into heavy weather. And "soundness" from the business angle means a minimum of interference with the established practices of commercial and industrial enterprise. The way of an innovating president, who is anxious for massive social legislation, is not likely to be strewn with roses.

This generalization is proved not only by the experience of Franklin Roosevelt. It is remarkably exemplified by the career of Mark Hanna; he was nothing so much as the business agent of capitalism in the Senate and at the White House in the later years of his career.[23] It is shown by the problems Theodore Roosevelt confronted when he sought to deal with conservation and the trusts. It is shown, again, by the fact that though the revelations of the Pujo Committee in 1913 depicted a situation of which the outcome was clearly prophesied at the time by Mr. Justice Brandeis,[24] nothing was done about it until the depression of 1929 put a new driving force behind the urgency of reform; and even now, it is a problem to know how far the substance of the legislation passed as a result of the Black Committee is likely to be permanent in its influence. An innovating president may appeal against the business criteria of "soundness" to public opinion. In an emergency period he is likely to obtain wide support for his attitude. But he is in the difficulty that the continuance of this support depends, to a considerable degree, upon his power to obtain the conditions of economic revival; and this power, in its turn, depends upon his ability to secure that co-operation from business men

[23] Cf. Herbert Croly, *Mark Hanna* (1912), for an illuminating picture of his views and activities.
[24] See his now-classic exposé, *Other People's Money* (1915).

which, by definition almost, his reform program repels. It is significant, for example, that Franklin Roosevelt's rearmament program evoked widespread assent from business men because it is a classic form of expenditure upon public works to which they are habituated by tradition. But expenditure on the experiments of the Works Progress Administration, of which the social value has been literally inestimable, has been bitterly denounced from its inception, rarely upon any factual basis, and mainly because its assumptions run counter to those of the classic form.

What I am concerned to show is that the "inarticulate major premises" of the presidential office limit by definition the area within which the president is free to move. The position itself imposes boundaries of action upon him. He is limited as to the men he may use as the instruments of his policy. He is limited by the interplay of the institutions with which he must cooperate. He is limited by the division of powers which the Constitution imposes, and the interpretation which is likely to be placed on the implications of that division by the courts. He is limited by the fact that he must conciliate his party and cannot coerce it; to be too far ahead of its conceptions is necessarily to court defeat. He is limited by the need to carry with him the members of a business community whose strategic position gives to it an economic and psychological authority unexampled, I think, in any other country in the world. To transcend these limitations either the president must be, like Lincoln, a supremely great man, or he must inherit an emergency, like war, as with Woodrow Wilson, or economic chaos, like Franklin Roosevelt, which so act upon public opinion as to suspend the normal assumptions of the American system.

And there is one other limitation to which attention must be directed. In a sense, the category of time is more important to the president of the United States than to any other political leader in the world. His term of office is for four years. But at the end of two, he is faced with a congressional election, in which the results of his policy are judged. He has, therefore, if he wants to make an impact upon the electoral mind, to do so with extraordinary rapidity. To be successful, indeed, he ought really to come into office with a pretty clear notion of the lines upon which he is to act. He has only six months between nomination and election; only eight months between nomination and accession to office. In five of these, the campaign, with its fatiguing journeys and endless speeches, is necessarily the first consideration; in the remaining three, he is the predestined victim of every important person and interest requiring consideration. After the mid-term congressional election, he has to make arrangements for his re-election, if he can. The whole impetus, accordingly, of the second half of his first term is set in the perspective of that necessity. Granted that he is likely to secure it—a refusal of the party to renominate is taken as a confession of failure—he has still to be careful lest he offend the powerful by his policy. And if he secures renomination, he is faced by the knowledge of two facts: there is, first, the mid-congressional election, with all its hazards, of his second term, and there is the virtual certainty that, two years later, he will have done with office forever. John Quincy Adams is the only president who, so far, has played a significant part in politics after leaving the White House. The knowledge, accordingly, that the scepter must pass from him, at the furthest, at the close of his second term operates decisively to weaken his influence in the last two years of his reign. Few presidents have had any substantial results to show during that period.

This raises the very interesting question of the proper length of the presidential term. The present limitation to two terms is, of course, simply a convention born of Washington's decision to retire at that stage. Had he wished for a third nomination, he could have had it, and Gouverneur Morris is only one of many who urged him strongly to continue. So far, no president has secured a third term, though it is possible that Jefferson and Jackson might have had it if they had wished. Grant eagerly desired a third term, but the strength of tradition and the dubious persons with whom he had surrounded himself while in office prevented his nomination. Theodore Roosevelt practically, though not technically, ran for a third term, but he did not secure the official nomination of his party. Certainly the pressure of public opinion against a third term is very strong. There is not only the power of tradition, in a country where tradition exercises very great authority. There is an important truth in the argument of Pro-

[65]

fessor Cushman that "the American people would grow very restive under a long, executive term of office . . . the change for which they so loudly clamor every four years is a safety valve for their prejudices and sentiments."[25]

It is clear, I think, that a single four-year term does not give elbowroom, especially when the danger of a loss of control of Congress at the mid-term election is remembered, to a president who has a big program in view. The persuasion of a democracy to big changes is at best a slow process, and a relatively small part of the president's time can be given to that purpose. This was seen by de Tocqueville a century ago. "It is impossible to consider," he wrote,[26] "the ordinary course of affairs in the United States without perceiving that the desire to be re-elected is the chief aim of the president; that his whole administration, and even his most indifferent measures, tend to this object; and that, as the crisis approaches, his personal interest takes the place of his interest in the public good." Nor is he in better case if he has decided not to run for a second term. Polk made that decision, and a revealing passage in his *Diary* shows the result of that self-denying ordinance. "With a large nominal majority in both houses," he wrote[27] about mid-way in his term, "I am practically in a minority. The several cliques and sections of the Democratic Party are manifestly more engaged in managing for their respective

[25] S. P. Orth and R. E. Cushman, *American National Government* (1931), p. 246.
[26] *Democracy in America* (ed. 1900), pp. 1, 136.
[27] *Diary of James K. Polk* (ed. Nevins, 1929), p. 186.

favorites in the next presidential election than they are in supporting the government in prosecuting the [Mexican] war, or in carrying out any of its great measures. The only corrective is in the hands of the people."

Four years is, clearly, too short a period of office in the light of the circumstances confronted by the president; and it has the great disadvantage that, without re-eligibility, it gives him the advantage of an experience of which it would then deprive the American people. But if there is to be, as there now is, re-eligibility, the difficulty de Tocqueville noted is an important consideration; the president, as John Randolph said in the convention,[28] "should not be left under a temptation to court a re-appointment." It is this which led Chief Justice Taft to suggest a change in the present system. "I am strongly inclined to the view," he wrote,[29] "that it would have been a wiser provision, as it was at one time voted in the convention, to make the term of the president six or seven years, and render him ineligible thereafter. Such a change would give to the executive greater courage and independence in the discharge of his duties. The absorbing and diverting interest in the re-election of the incumbent, taken by those federal civil servants who regard their own tenure as dependent upon his, would disappear and the efficiency of administration in the last eighteen months of a term would be maintained."

[28] Farrand, *Records of the Federal Convention*, I, pp. 104 f.
[29] *Our Chief Magistrate and His Powers* (1916), p. 4.

It is, I think, difficult to read the documents without the conviction that Mr. Taft was right. If there is to be no re-eligibility, a term of four years is too short; if there is to be re-elegibility, the argument against a third term is not a very convincing one. The fear of monarchy which pervaded the mind of some, at least, of the founders is no longer valid; the fear of Caesarism uttered by contemporary critics omits the vital fact that the whole framework of the American scheme of government is utterly incompatible with Caesarism. A Caesar, if some crisis led to his emergence in the United States, would have to do far more than is implied in mere re-election upon the basis of the present presidential powers. The true and only issue involved in the problem of a third term is whether, on a balance of considerations, the American people want any given incumbent who offers himself; and that, after all, is a question which the American people alone are competent to decide.

There are, of course, important considerations to be weighed. The burden of the office is very heavy, especially in critical times; few men could easily carry it for more than eight years. It needs an incumbent who is at the height of his powers. A president must be thirty-five; but he is, as a rule, in early middle age on election. An eight-year period of office brings him near to the middle sixties; after that, the strain begins to tell if it is borne continuously. On the other hand, there are exceptional men who bear the years with relative indifference, Mr. Gladstone, for instance, and Bismarck. Peel was seventy when he was killed;

and there was no evidence of any decline in his powers. From this angle, the whole problem is clearly individual to the man, and all generalizations are out of place.

It is, indeed, true that democracy is based on the thesis that no man is indispensable; therein lies one of its most vital differences from a dictatorial regime, which usually finds insoluble the problem of the succession to the dictator. But here, the electorate has its own remedy; it has the power to choose or not to choose the given incumbent for a further term as it will. If, patently, he seems superior to any alternative, it must seem to the outsider a grievous waste of human resources to put a president on the shelf mainly because, for private reasons, George Washington decided to serve for two terms only. The power to plan, the experience gained, the stability of personnel established, the sense acquired by the nation of continuity in direction—all these are valuable assets, if they cohere about the right person. To discard them for a mechanical formula is to miss altogether the central essence of what government requires. Part of the virtue of popular choice lies in its ability to keep the right man when it has found him. Certainly a good deal of the merit of the British system has lain in the full utilization of that capacity. To argue otherwise is, I think, to argue in favor of a single-term system. The case for that method is, no doubt, a strong one. But the case against it is the decisive one that it is not the method upon which the presidential office has been built.

II

THE PRESIDENT AND HIS CABINET

I

ALMOST from the outset of Washington's administration, the executive heads of departments
began to assume the character of a cabinet; and the
fact that it is so referred to by name in Marshall's
decision in *Marbury* v. *Madison*[1] is proof enough that
it had already become an integral part of the institutional framework of the United States. But it is important to realize at once that the American cabinet
hardly corresponds to the classic idea of a cabinet to
which representative government in Europe has accustomed us.

Its members, of course, cannot, under the Constitution, be members of either house of Congress; and
tradition, which perhaps goes back to Jefferson's fear
of Hamilton's powers of persuasion, prevents them
from taking part in debate there. Cabinet officers in
the United States are essentially presidential advisers.
They may give information to Congress. They may
appear before committees in defense of the measures
they have recommended. They may make public
speeches in support of the general policy of the ad-

[1] (1803) 1 Cranch 137.

ministration. They may even initiate a line of policy which, granted presidential approval, is recognized as their own special contribution to affairs; so the agricultural policy of Mr. Wallace and the reciprocal low-tariff agreements of Mr. Hull are associated, in Franklin Roosevelt's administration, with a line of thought to which each of these ministers attaches special significance. But, in general, the American cabinet minister lives and moves and has his being in the context of presidential thought. However able and distinguished, he is bound to be eclipsed by the major significance of his chief.

It is, indeed, rare for a majority of any given cabinet to have outstanding importance in the political life of America. The composition of a cabinet is unpredictable. Many of its members, after their term of office, retire into the obscurity from which their elevation brought them. It is comparatively rare for a figure of outstanding distinction in Congress, at least since the Civil War, to choose cabinet office in preference to the continuance of his congressional career; and this is true even though men like Clay and Webster, Calhoun and Blaine, Bryan and Root served in this capacity. The office has rarely served, since Jackson's time, as a highroad to the presidency. Membership is rather a phase in a life-career; it is not itself an integral part of a career. No one thought of Mr. Newton D. Baker as a possible secretary of war before 1916; and, though he was a possible candidate for the Democratic nomination in 1932, he held no national office before or after that four years' interlude in his law practice. Miss Perkins was well known in New York before she became secretary of labor in 1933; but she had never possessed an important political position before that time. In the British and the French systems, cabinet office is the goal toward which a member of the legislative assembly seeks continually to move; accession to it is the crown of a political career. With Americans, this is not the case; and it may even be said that there is no special reason why the fact that a man has attained cabinet rank should assure him any pivotal part in the political world.

That is shown in many ways. Not only does the resignation of a cabinet member make little or no difference to the strength of the president's position; it is almost assumed that some members of the cabinet will resign during his term. Nor is it likely that, because a man is in the cabinet, he will, thereby, exercise influence with Congress; on the record, it is rare for this to be the case unless he has previously been a member of either house, and popular there. To bring a man from the back benches of the House to the cabinet in England is at once to clothe any announcement he may make with definite importance; but a speech, say, of the chairman of the Senate Committee on Foreign Affairs will always rival in significance any utterance that may be made even by the secretary of state. A prime minister in England or in France hazards his head when he dispenses with a powerful colleague; Lord John Russell did not long survive his dismissal of Palmerston in 1851. And an

English politician who refuses cabinet office may thereby risk bringing his effective political career to a close—as Sir Robert (now Viscount) Horne did when he refused to become minister of labor in Mr. Baldwin's government of 1925. But a president does not have to consider the danger of dispensing with a powerful colleague just because, from his angle, he has no powerful colleagues in the cabinet who may jeopardize his position. A politician does not take risks by refusing cabinet office, if he already has national prestige on other grounds; Senator Glass could have been secretary of the treasury in 1933. But everyone understood the grounds upon which he preferred to stay in the Senate.

The cabinet is a body of advisers to the president; it is not a council of colleagues with whom he has to work and upon whose approval he depends. There is, indeed, as a rule, a weekly cabinet meeting at which discussion takes place upon those issues the president wishes to raise. But there is no collective responsibility. Issues of the gravest importance need not be, indeed are not, submitted to the cabinet at all; Franklin Roosevelt went forward with his Court plan without most of the cabinet's having any knowledge of it. Even a united cabinet cannot prevail against the will of the president. There is hardly a department in which the direction of, and initiative in, policy is not his if he wants to assume them. He is a court of appeal from them all, and his verdict is decisive against them. They make, collectively, no impact upon Congress or the nation, as he does; their relation is one of departmental interstitiality. No doubt some of them are in a position to influence his decisions; they are never in a position to control them. A member of the cabinet differs from the president at his peril. Even so renowned a party leader as Mr. Bryan never recovered from the consequences of his resignation. After 1915, he never exerted the influence that was previously his. A cabinet officer, normally, must assume that he will live his term in the presidential shadow. What substance is his depends upon the will of the president.

It is, of course, true that the relation varies. A weak president, like Buchanan or Harding, gives far more leeway to his colleagues, sometimes with disastrous results. A strong president may place special reliance upon a particular colleague; Lincoln did upon Stanton and Theodore Roosevelt upon Elihu Root. But Mr. Wilson, in all matters of major importance, treated his secretaries of state like office boys; and it is clear that the vital initiative in all major matters has lain with the White House under Franklin Roosevelt. How impossible it is for a cabinet officer, however eminent, to control a president who has made up his mind was shown by the relations between Lincoln and Seward. The latter was far more widely known than the president when he took office, was, indeed, far more experienced; and it is clear that he hoped to act as a kind of tutelary deity to a man whose inferiority he did not hesitate to assume. He was rapidly undeceived; and, from first to last, every major action of the State Department bears the mark of Lincoln's own hand.

Polk, too, rode his cabinet on a tight rein; and his *Diary* makes it clear that he had never any doubt who was master. Under Coolidge, on the other hand, at least three of the cabinet shaped the lines of their policy with but little interference from the president; though the incisiveness of his control, when he thought the credit of his government was at stake, is shown clearly enough by his dismissal of his attorney-general.[2]

Not only is the initiative in policy a matter for presidential discretion. In areas of supreme importance a president may rely upon councilors who have, technically, no official status at all. As early as the thirties of last century, Andrew Jackson had his "kitchen cabinet," which was far more influential with him than his official family. None of Mr. Wilson's colleagues ever carried with him the weight of authority of Colonel House. Mark Hanna had much the position of House at the height of his power; and it is probable that not more than two of Franklin Roosevelt's colleagues have ever had the weight of half a dozen advisers outside. Alongside this, the American system makes it almost inevitable that the leaders of his party in both houses of Congress, and especially the Senate, should have an authority with the president to which no cabinet officer can pretend. It is upon them that he must depend for the passage of his measures. In face of their recalcitrance he is lost, where he can always overcome the obstinacy of a cabinet member. Vis-à-vis Congress, indeed, the

[2] William Allen White, *A Puritan in Babylon* (1938), pp. 271-272.

president may be said to be dealing with something akin to a shadow-cabinet which argues with him on terms far more approaching equality than the official cabinet can hope to do.

This is intelligible enough, from one angle. The leaders of Congress ought to exercise great influence for the simple reason that they are charged with an independent responsibility. To the foreigner, the influence of the unofficial advisers is more startling. They are not, necessarily, politicians of standing, nor expert in the subject matter with which they deal. Colonel House, on the evidence, seems to have been a simple, rather vain man, with a great affection for Mr. Wilson, and an immense liking for the kind of diplomacy in which he could exercise influence without responsibility. For a brief period, a Professor Warren, whose specialism was agriculture, persuaded President Franklin Roosevelt to embark upon a disastrous currency experiment of immense magnitude. Professor Moley was, indeed, the undersecretary of the State Department; but, if his own account be accurate, for the first fifteen months of Franklin Roosevelt's first administration he exercised more authority over the president than all his cabinet together;[3] though it must be added that his own account makes it clear that the phases of policy in which he played his part were determined by the president. The problem created by these unofficial advisers is clearly the twofold one that they have no responsibility for the advice they give, and their hour of authority depends

[3] See his account of his appointment, *After Seven Years* (1939).

upon their ability to persuade the president to listen to them. In Colonel House's case, that ability mainly took the form of advising the president to act in the way he intuitively guessed the president wished to act. The famous break of 1919, which he always declared he did not understand, obviously arose from the fact that, at the Peace Conference, he passed beyond that function and began to act as though he were an independent agent. Such positions, in fact, are comparable to those of a favorite at Court; and it is, I think, wholly undesirable that they should reach as far as Colonel House made his effort go. For, out of them, as his papers show, there arise understandings, and even commitments, which are not of the kind to be made by unofficial agents, especially when these are unknown to those who are called officially to assist the president in the making of policy.

2

This position of the cabinet arises from the conditions under which it has to be made. An English prime minister, when he assumes office, is largely given the men upon whom he must rely. Disraeli must have Cairns; Gladstone must have Hartington; Campbell-Bannerman must have Asquith. The party expects certain men to be in the cabinet; the country, also, expects them to be there. No doubt the prime minister, once he has passed beyond certain obvious peaks, has a real discretion; Mr. Baldwin's choice of Mr. Churchill as chancellor of the exchequer in 1925 was a surprise; so, also, was Mr. Chamberlain's choice of Lord Chatfield as minister for the co-ordination of defense in 1939. But Mr. Churchill, after all, had been for nearly twenty years a distinguished figure in British politics; and Lord Chatfield was an eminent naval officer chosen for a post in which his special *expertise* had peculiar relevance at the time when he was called.

The attorney-general apart, it is rare for any American cabinet officer to have any special claims to the post he fills. There are, of course, exceptions; the appointment of Mr. Henry Wallace to the Department of Agriculture in 1933 was—apart from the fact that his previous party connections were Republican—natural in the light of his position as one of the outstanding editors of an agricultural paper in America. But the considerations a president must have in mind as he forms his cabinet are quite different from those a British or a French prime minister must have in mind. The latter, first of all, is building a team whose basic purpose is the maintenance of unity as a team. Most of them have been well known to Parliament for a considerable period. Most of them, also, have acted in opposition as a shadow-cabinet and know one another's ways. Many of them, normally, will have held office before and will be accustomed to the habits of public administration. All of them can rely upon a skilled collaboration from the civil service; and many of them will know with some intimacy the high officials with whom they are going to collaborate.

Little of this position confronts the president. He

is not, in the first place, making a team. Some of his colleagues may hardly be known to him when he chooses them; some of them, at least, will not be known at all to one another. He must have one or two men who are likely to be influential with Congress; the choice of a Calhoun or a Webster or a Clay becomes at once explicable on this ground. One, at least, must be a person directly expert in the handling of the party machine; Mr. Walter Brown, under President Hoover, Mr. Farley, under Franklin Roosevelt, obviously fills the role. There must be representatives of the territorial sections of the country; a cabinet constructed wholly of Easterners would be offensive to the West and the South. There ought, desirably, to be representatives of the predominant religions of the United States; a prominent Methodist and an outstanding Catholic layman will always make presidential relations more easy. It is said that Theodore Roosevelt made Mr. Oscar Straus the secretary of commerce in the belief that this would incline the support of the large Jewish vote in America toward the Republicans. It has been usual for the secretary of labor to be chosen from the ranks of important trade unionists; and it is notable that this custom caused President Franklin Roosevelt some little difficulty when he ignored it to appoint Miss Frances Perkins in that office. Her choice is interesting, since it may well compel a future president to include a woman in the cabinet as a measure designed to please the women in America, not least in view of their powerful organization in such bodies as the League of Women Voters.

But this is not all. A president has also to pay for his nomination and election. Mr. Wilson, obviously enough, selected Mr. Bryan as his secretary of state as a reward for the latter's decision to support him as against Mr. Champ Clark in the Democratic convention of 1912. Cleveland chose Gresham as his secretary of state, though he was a Republican, and a former member of President Arthur's cabinet, in order to gratify the low-tariff Republicans who had become "Mugwumps." President Harding rewarded his campaign manager, Mr. Harry Daugherty, with the office of attorney-general—an appointment as disastrous as any in the history of modern administrations. Mr. Mellon's contribution to the Republican campaign fund in 1920 was largely responsible for his choice as secretary of the treasury. McKinley and Theodore Roosevelt both gave gold-Democrats places in their cabinets to mark their gratitude to men who supported them as a protest against the danger of "Bryanism" among their opponents. At the end of his administration Mr. Wilson appointed Mr. Bainbridge Colby, a Republican, as successor to Mr. Lansing in the State Department in a vain effort to persuade some of the Republicans to help him force the Versailles Treaty upon the Senate.

It is a tradition, broken only once in modern times,[4] that the presidential appointments to the cabinet should

[4] In 1925 when the Senate refused twice to ratify Mr. Coolidge's choice of Mr. Charles B. Warren as his attorney-general.

be confirmed by the Senate; it is rightly felt that the president had better choose the men with whom he has to live. And, political expediency apart, the personal view of the president always plays a considerable part in the selection of his colleagues. The choice of Mr. Hull and Mr. Swanson by President Franklin Roosevelt was obviously dictated by political considerations; on the other hand, that of Mr. Woodin, for the Treasury, of Mr. Ickes for the Interior, of Miss Perkins for Labor, were obviously definitely personal appointments. So, at a later stage, was the appointment of Mr. Morgenthau to succeed Mr. Woodin on the latter's death. So, also, was that of Mr. Hopkins to succeed Mr. Roper in the Department of Commerce. Mr. Hopkins' appointment, indeed, was in a sense an outstanding example of the tradition which gives the president free play. Mr. Hopkins, until 1932, was a social worker of some distinction, but of no very definite political leanings. He came under the notice of Mr. Roosevelt and was chosen to head the Works Progress Administration. In that position, he grew rapidly into perhaps the closest adviser of the president, certainly his most intimate friend; and his elevation to the cabinet was nothing so much as a signal mark of personal friendship made in order to answer passionate criticism of Mr. Hopkins which emanated hardly less from the president's own party than it did from his opponents. Hardly less interesting was the choice of the attorney-general in 1939. It had long been expected that Mr. Cummings' resignation would be followed by the appointment of the solicitor-general, Mr. Robert Jackson, whose work, both as lawyer and as politician, had been of exceptional distinction. But Mr. Roosevelt nominated Mr. Frank Murphy, a former governor of Michigan, who had just been defeated in his contest for re-election, despite the special support of the president. It is not, I think, unfair to suppose that Mr. Jackson was passed over as a result of the president's desire to mark in an exceptional way the confidence and regard he had for Mr. Murphy.

On the whole it is true, I believe, to say that a Democratic cabinet contains more surprises than a Republican cabinet, especially in recent years. This is largely because the divisions within the parties have grown wider. Anyone who studies the relations, for example, between the progressive Republicans and their more conservative colleagues for the last twenty-five years will have some difficulty in believing that the same party label can cover men of such divergent views. Presidents, not unnaturally, have sought to take advantage of these differences. Cleveland's appointment of Gresham, and Franklin Roosevelt's appointment of Mr. Ickes may, I think, not unfairly be represented as attempts to assure themselves support which would transcend the normal differences between parties. For the allegiance of the voter is a pretty shifting thing. An unexpected appointment, whether in terms of party, or section, or even religious creed, may make a considerable difference to the hold a president has upon his volatility.

What is striking in the result that emerges is how

little can be known of the administrative capacity of
cabinet members, whether as individuals, or as a team,
until they have got under way. They have rarely, as
a team, had continuity of contact with great affairs.
They have not learned to be a unity in the sense that
the members of an English cabinet are a unity before
they begin their work. Some of them, even, do not
know either their chief or one another, except in the
most casual way, until they find themselves in office.
They come and go upon grounds which not seldom
are very different from those to which a European
is accustomed. At the end of 1938, for example, the
attorney-general resigned in order, by a return to
legal practice, to recoup his personal fortunes. And
only a minority has any serious hold upon the outside
public. Not more than one or two can speak in the
name of the administration in the sense in which an
English cabinet minister can. For the most part, also,
the substance of their speeches tends to be narrowly
departmental in character. Mr. Ickes or Mr. Hull may
take a roving commission in discourse; Mr. Farley
may, as chairman of the National Democratic Committee, generalize upon the wider aspects of policy.
But the American public would be surprised if Miss
Perkins, as secretary of labor, suddenly spoke her
full mind upon international affairs, or if Mr. Morgenthau, as secretary of the treasury, were to express
his views upon the conflict between the A. F. of L.
and the C. I. O. In the main, generalizations are a
presidential prerogative; and it is not customary for

[83]

the cabinet officer to think at all profoundly over a wide field.

This does not mean that the president does not consult his cabinet; the documents make it plain that he does so with some continuity. But they suggest that the technique of cabinet functioning is not a pooling of the minds in the British or French sense. It is not merely that the president is always free to make his own decisions; it is not merely, either, that he always tends to develop a special relation with one or two intimates in a cabinet, as Theodore Roosevelt did with Elihu Root. It is that cabinet discussion is the collection of opinions by the president with a view to clarifying his own mind, rather than a search for a collective decision. A cabinet officer may resent a presidential determination about which he has not been consulted, as Mr. Root is said[5] to have resented Theodore Roosevelt's decision to prosecute, under the Sherman Act, the Northern Securities case; but he is not entitled to resent it and his resentment has no effective remedy. For if he resigns, as Mr. Wilson's secretary of war resigned, because he disagrees with presidential policy, he normally retires into obscurity without in any serious way affecting the position or policy the president may choose to follow.

How complete is the absence of collective responsibility was strikingly shown in the oil scandals under President Harding. Three members of the cabinet were concerned; all of them were compelled to resign; two of them were criminally indicted, and one

[5] H. F. Pringle, *Theodore Roosevelt* (1931), p. 255.

of them served a prison sentence. The matter in which they were involved raised issues of high policy; and it was passionately discussed in Congress and the press. Yet it seems, throughout, to have been treated as an interdepartmental matter upon which any decision, when public opinion became involved, was a presidential prerogative. Mr. Hoover, who was later the president of the United States, and Mr. Hughes, who was later to become its chief justice, were both members of the cabinet throughout its operative period. Neither seems ever to have concerned himself with the issue, or to have regarded it as one with which he was concerned; nor did the public treat it as one in which their honor was in any way involved. Yet it is inconceivable that a similar situation in England, in which, say, the three defence ministers were parties to a corrupt bargain that became a theme of intense public discussion, would not have its impact upon the status of the cabinet as a whole. And this aloofness is not novel, for it is, in its way, a reproduction of a similar scandal in the cabinet of President Grant.

The decisions of the cabinet are thus in the nature of advice to the president rather than a corporate act. Anyone who reads the letters of Theodore Roosevelt, or the documents we now possess about the Wilson administration, will see how largely this is the case. The cabinet officer may well expect to be consulted about his own department, though he has no assurance that his advice will be taken; he does not know that he will be generally consulted, and he has no title to general consultation. He may find himself no better informed upon a momentous decision before it has been taken than a member of the ordinary public; and he may find that an important senator or congressman is regarded as far more relevant than he is to the process which leads to its making. Not many of Mr. Wilson's cabinet can have been aware of the intimate substance of Colonel House's vital negotiations with Sir E. Grey in 1915-16, still less that the president's mind was made up, as early as 1916, to intervene, if need be, to prevent the defeat of the allies. It may well be that awareness would have resulted in their agreement; certainly their published memoirs suggest that this would have been the case. But, as a cabinet, they were not taking part in the making of policies; they were accepting decisions already arrived at in the presidential mind. And they had no alternative but to accept them.

In this situation, it is intelligible enough that, as a career, membership in the cabinet does not compare with that of a senator. The latter has a sphere of influence in which, so long as he secures re-election, he is his own master, and he has a platform second only to that of the president from which to address the nation. It may be doubted whether any cabinet officer, in the period since Hamilton was the secretary of the treasury, has had the influence or the attention of Senator Aldrich or of Senator Borah. One has only to compare the trembling uncertainty of John Hay about his tenure of the Department of State after the assassination of McKinley, with Senator Norris' rugged defiance of Harding and Coolidge to realize the difference in position. Few presidents are likely to consult their cabinet colleagues with any continuity about, for example, judicial appointments; but it is well known that Senator Borah's influence was decisive in placing Mr. Justice Cardozo on the Supreme Court, and it is believed that Senator Norris played an important part in the nomination of Mr. Justice Frankfurter—in this case against the pressure of President Roosevelt's first attorney-general. And, of course, where senatorial courtesy is concerned, the Senate will act as a unit against the president to enforce that consideration of a colleague which it considers his due.

Cabinet office, this is to say, is an interlude in a career; it is not itself a career. There is no technique of direct preparation for it; there is no certainty that it will continue because it has begun; there is no assurance that the successful performance of its functions will lead to a renewal of office in a subsequent administration. It is, no doubt, an exaggeration to say that the cabinet officer is simply the president's man in charge of a particular department; but it is not an exaggeration to say that he must be prepared, without repining or resigning, to be the president's man on any particular point about which the president is adamant. He does not increase his political influence, when he differs from his chief, by resigning in order to appeal beyond him to public opinion; for his position is such that there is no public opinion to which he may appeal. He does not even make himself available as a presidential candidate by successful administration. Where a cabinet officer, like Clay or Taft or Mr. Hoover, has attained this position, his cabinet reputation has been but a small factor in his nomination. If, indeed, a cabinet officer has presidential ambitions, he is more likely than not to arouse the suspicions of the president unless, as with Taft and Theodore Roosevelt, the president has determined to push his candidature. "No candidate for the presidency," wrote James K. Polk,[6] "ought ever to remain in the cabinet. He is an unsafe adviser." That is a view that any president is likely to take if the aspirant's convictions differ from his own. For, save in exceptional cases, he is bound to feel that the advice he is offered is governed less by the evidence than by the cabinet officer's judgment of its effect upon his chances of the nomination. That view is not easily compatible with an honest and disinterested relationship.[7]

The truth is that the relation between the president and his cabinet, however harmonious, does not seriously diminish the burden which rests upon the former; and, above all, it does not relieve him in the vital realm of foreign affairs. Partly, this is the case simply because in the last resort the cabinet is not a responsible body; it is the president, and the president alone, who is responsible for its actions. But partly, also, it is not, like its European analogues, a policy-making body; every major item of affairs ultimately is settled by the president's view of what is desirable.

---

[6] *Diary of James K. Polk* (ed. Nevins, 1929), p. 308.
[7] Cf. Polk's view, *ibid.*, p. 64 (Buchanan) and p. 72 (Calhoun).

Partly, further, the result of this concentration of power in the president's hands is to make him, almost necessarily, a court of appeal from departmental decisions wherever the person appealing is powerful enough to have direct influence in the White House. An important member of either house of Congress, a powerful commercial interest, a great trade union, can always feel pretty confident that he will have the opportunity, if he is dissatisfied with a departmental decision, of stating his case directly to the president. In a sense, indeed, an appeal of this kind is almost a matter of common form. An American citizen of standing would hardly feel that his case had been properly dealt with unless its ultimate disposition had been a matter of presidential thought.

That is because collective cabinet responsibility does not exist; the matter disposed of is always one the form of which it is assumed the president may shape differently from his adviser. And he may well so shape it. It may be an appointment to the Supreme Court; it may be the stabilization of international currencies; it may be the attitude of the administration to some pivotal point in labor policy. It is not, I think, too much to say that a large proportion of business that in England would be disposed of departmentally, that, even if submitted directly to the prime minister, would be remitted by him for ultimate disposal by a cabinet colleague, is, in the United States, business not merely that the president will decide, but also that he will be expected to decide. The relief, therefore, that he can expect from his colleagues is far smaller than it is in England. And if it were not smaller, the whole system would be very different from what it is. The expectation of direct thought from the president by the citizen-body of the United States is greater than the analogous expectation of any similar citizen-body elsewhere. In England, we blame an anonymous entity "the Government" if things go wrong, or a mistake is made; in the United States it is the president who is blamed. A decision of the Supreme Court is regarded as adverse to *his* policy; a defeat in Congress is a blow to *his* prestige; the mid-term congressional elections affect *his* policy, for good or ill. No one thinks of them in terms of their effect upon his cabinet. For the purpose of action, it is he alone who is fundamentally involved.

The temptation is to say that the result is to place upon the shoulders of the president a burden greater than any man can be asked to bear. In a sense, no doubt, this is unquestionably the case. The range of issues he may be called upon to handle is by all odds greater than any man can hope, or be expected, to handle wisely, and there is rarely the kind of consideration available to him that he needs for a wise judgment. He lacks the kind of *expertise* the civil servants of an English department will, for the most part, place at the disposal of their minister. He lacks, from most of his cabinet, the kind of counsel that comes from men who are equally sharing with him in the adventure of government. The colleagueship of the leaders of his party in Congress, even supposing his party to be in a majority, is not, as the record shows plainly, of that intimate character which relieves the sense of perpetual strain under which any president must live. And most presidential correspondence reveals that sense of strain. It emerges not only in the letters and diaries of men who, like Lincoln, were engaged in dealing with a crisis of the first magnitude. It emerges, also, with presidents whose path, like that of Taft, was relatively smooth. Whatever the intimacies a president may build, he is ultimately a lonely figure. The burden of office is, in a special sense, his and his only; there is no one who can share it with him, or take it from him. He is not a dictator, whose will is certain to be imposed upon his followers. He is not even sure, like a prime minister, that in the absence of major blunders he can maintain his hold upon his party. His position makes him a target to be attacked by every person or interest at all critical of his purposes. He is there, in all cases, to be blamed; and there is no one, in any real sense, who can help him to bear the burden of the blame.

Part of this, no doubt, is due to the nature of politicians; part of it has been shaped by the history of the office; and part of it is due, I think, to the psychological habits of the American people. The politician, almost by definition, is a person eager for power. He is a man who is anxious that his will should prevail against other and competing wills. The presidency gives to men of this temper an opportunity of which, unless they are weak in will, they are almost bound to take full advantage. Even an easy-going president, like Taft, who did not himself want the office,[8] is almost driven by its immanent logic to attempt a leadership the maintenance of which means that, when differences occur, he must make his own decisions. And that attitude is reinforced by the nature of the presidency. He is the only person, on the executive side, who holds an independent position; his cabinet officers, however eminent, are there because he has willed that they shall be there. However eminent, they hold office at his pleasure; they must go whenever he decides that he no longer wants their co-operation. They lack, that is to say, that sense of being necessary to the strength of the president which an important English cabinet officer has. Mr. Lloyd George in the Asquith government, Mr. Chamberlain in that of Mr. Baldwin, Sir William Harcourt in that of Lord Rosebery, Mr. Arthur Henderson in the first and second governments of Mr. Ramsay MacDonald, had each an independent position in the eyes of the nation; with the American cabinet officer such independence is so rare as to be almost a negligible factor in its operation. He cannot hope to break the president; it is even rare for him to be able to injure his prestige. No one is in a position to enforce an alternative view against him save Congress. For the years, in short, in which he holds office the denials he must face, the criticisms he must encounter, are always external to the executive power; they are never inherent in it.

And so momentous is the internal prestige of the office that internal denials and criticisms never come to him in such a way as to assure that the full weight of

[8] Pringle, *op. cit.*, p. 498.

their inner logic will be attached to them. The men who are playing for presidential influence on their side, within the framework of the executive power, are never certain that they will carry it just because they are members of the cabinet. That is clear, for instance, in foreign policy. No one can read Polk's own account of the Mexican War without the realization that, though he may have listened to the advice of his cabinet, the real motive-power to action was, throughout, a policy upon which he himself had made up his mind. That was true, also, of Lincoln; it was true of Woodrow Wilson; and it seems pretty clear that, when the documents are available, it will be true also of Franklin Roosevelt. Indeed, there is a sense in which the more positive and independent the affirmations of the president, the more, so to say, the springs of his policy are in himself, rather than shared with others, the profounder will be the impact he makes upon the national life. A president who is believed not to make up his own mind rapidly loses the power to maintain that hold. The need to dramatize his position by insistence upon his undoubted supremacy is inherent in the office as history has shaped it. A masterful man in the White House will, under all circumstances, be more to the liking of the multitude than one who is thought to be swayed by his colleagues. Even when, as with Theodore Roosevelt, great verbal audacity is accompanied by a relative caution in action, the mere fact that the president insists upon being the center of the stage continuously strengthens his position. It is, it should be added, an attitude that is expected of him.

For the president is news, in a way that cannot be said of any member of his cabinet. Every action of his will be reported; his lightest word, almost, is discussed and repeated, and the last ounce of possible meaning extracted from it. That is not the case with the cabinet. Its members must take steps to bring themselves before the public; and, even if they are successful in doing so, they must be content to live under the presidential shadow. It is even, I think, true to say that whereas the criticism that a president may evoke is to some extent restrained by the very fact that he is the president—the resemblance here to a member of the British royal family is notable—no such restraint is deemed incumbent upon the critics of a cabinet officer. And whereas the president's opinions are all of them, at least temporarily, significant, the cabinet officer must, for the most part, confine himself to his departmental functions if he wants to be heard. If Mr. Roosevelt chose to speak on American art, it is certain that a public discussion of his opinions would follow; but if the secretary of the treasury spoke on such a theme, most people would wonder why he strayed so far from the path of common sense. The president, in a word, symbolizes the whole nation in a way and to a degree that admits of no competitor while he is in office. Alongside his, the voice of a cabinet officer is, at best, a whisper, which may or may not be heard.

Indeed, what is striking in the American scene is

the number of voices, the president apart, which compete for attention with those of the cabinet officers. An outstanding banker, like the late J. P. Morgan, for example, will usually command not less attention than the secretary of the treasury in matters of finance; an eminent labor leader, like Mr. John L. Lewis, will at least rival in interest the opinions of the secretary of labor. The president of Harvard University has a national position which compares not unfavorably with that of any but the two or three outstanding cabinet officers. A great industrialist, like Mr. Ford, can make his pronouncements "news" in a sense that few cabinet members can rival, unless they are known to be speaking in the name of the president on some great public theme. None of them is likely to surpass in public significance a senator of any considerable standing; and a congressman who is either Speaker of the House, or the chairman of an important committee, has at least equal standing. My point is that his membership in the cabinet, as such, is never a guarantee either that he will make policy in any important way, or that he will assume a position of national significance by reason of it. The context in which he is set is that of presidential exigency; in that context he lives and moves and has his being.

That is true of the cabinet as a group of individuals; it is true, also, of the cabinet as a collective entity. During the war, President Wilson held no cabinet meetings; policy was made by him in the light of personal consultation with different members of it. Even after his return from Versailles, this continued to be the case. He was ill from September, 1919, until April, 1920, during which period no cabinet meeting was held. When a railroad strike seemed to call for such a meeting, Mr. Lansing, who, as secretary of state, was the senior member of the cabinet, called his colleagues together for consultation. He did so only after careful discussion, and because neither he nor they were allowed access to the president, and because no member of the cabinet was willing to take important action on his own initiative. Mr. Wilson's response to that action was summarily to dismiss Mr. Lansing. That was, on any showing, an extraordinary action, for there is not an atom of reason to suppose that Mr. Lansing was trying to do other than his best under very difficult circumstances. And even if we attribute Mr. Wilson's harshness in part to his natural arrogance and in part to the obvious petulance of a sick man, the fact that his action passed with but little criticism is sufficient proof of the degree to which presidential control defines the sphere of initiative within which the cabinet officer may hope to move. He originates at his peril.

3

This situation may be related to the effort, which goes back for three-quarters of a century, to secure the right to speak, though not, of course, to vote,[9] upon the floor of Congress. As long ago as February, 1864, Mr. Pendleton, a congressman from Ohio, sought to secure that "heads of executive departments

[9] Voting would, of course, be unconstitutional.

may occupy seats on the floor of the House of Representatives"; and his proposal was strongly supported by James A. Garfield, then also a congressman from Ohio, in a remarkable speech. The committee to which the resolution was referred then introduced a bill containing two proposals: (1) cabinet officers were to have the right, in their own discretion, to attend debates when matters concerning their departments were under discussion; and (2) their attendance was to be made compulsory on certain days for the purpose of answering questions.[10] An ardent discussion took place upon the bill, but it was not voted on. Fifteen years later, Pendleton, then a member of the Senate, raised the question a second time. The committee to which his resolution was referred produced a long and valuable report;[11] but, as in 1864, no vote was taken upon the proposed measure. In 1886, Mr. J. D. Long, later a secretary of the navy, introduced a measure which permitted members of the cabinet to attend and speak, at their own pleasure, in the House of Representatives; but, on this occasion, the bill was not reported out of committee. The proposal then slumbered for twenty-five years. It was revived by President Taft who supported the idea of cabinet representation in Congress with considerable vigor; but his proposal came to nothing. It was renewed in 1921 and 1924; in neither case did it arouse any serious public interest or discussion.

The case for the Pendleton proposal has been well

[10] House Rep. 43. 38th Congress, 1st Session (1864).
[11] Sen. Rep. 837. 46th Congress, 3rd Session (1881).

stated by President Taft. "Without any change in the Constitution," he wrote, "Congress might well provide that heads of departments, members of the president's cabinet, should be given access to the floor of each house to introduce measures, to advocate their passage, to answer questions, and to enter into the debate as if they were members, without, of course, the right to vote. . . . This would impose on the president greater difficulty in selecting his cabinet, and would lead him to prefer men of legislative experience who have shown their power to take care of themselves in legislative debate. It would stimulate the head of each department by the fear of public and direct inquiry into a more thorough familiarity with the actual operations of his department and into a closer supervision of its business. On the other hand, it would give the president what he ought to have, some direct initiative in legislation, and an opportunity, through the presence of his competent representatives in Congress, to keep each house advised of the facts in the actual operation of the government. The time lost in Congress over useless discussion of issues that might be disposed of by a single statement from the head of a department, no one can appreciate unless he has filled such a place."[12]

The case is obviously a powerful one; and it has had the support of men so experienced as Mr. Justice Story, Senator Ingalls, and James G. Blaine. The case is the stronger with the immense growth, in recent years, of the congressional appetite for information

[12] *Our Chief Magistrate and His Powers* (1916), p. 32.

from and investigation of the departments, much of which, if it is to be really effective, demands their friendly collaboration. There can be little doubt that it would greatly enhance the significance of congressional debate; and, thereby, it would give to it a character of responsibility and a popular significance which, compared to those of the House of Commons, are in considerable degree lacking. There is, too, much to be said for breaking down the antagonism between Congress and the departments; at present it is not untrue to say that many of the amendments each house makes to bills derive less from a knowledge of their value than from a desire to emphasize its power. I have myself heard Mr. Theodore Roosevelt insist that this method was not only likely to produce a wiser selection of cabinet officers; it was also, in his judgment, the best way to deal with the inherent difficulties of tariff legislation and of the "pork-barrel" bills which still remain a blot of no mean dimensions on the record of the legislature.

The argument, however, has not yet penetrated deeply into the popular consciousness. It is notable that in neither of his remarkable books on the American system did Woodrow Wilson think it worth while discussing, though he paid great attention to the relation between the executive and the legislature; while Lord Bryce, who knew Senator Pendleton personally, relegates it to a footnote in his *American Commonwealth*.[13] The reason, I think, is clear. The change is not a superficial one. Its ramifications are,

[13] *American Commonwealth* (ed. of 1911), I, 86.

in fact, so wide that they might easily change the whole balance of power in the American system. They might change it, not merely as between the executive and the legislature, but within the elements of the executive itself. The failure to give the plan the consideration it deserves is not, I think, due to inertia, but rather, as Professor Cushman rightly suggests,[14] to "the vaguely uneasy feeling that the plan would unwisely upset the traditional and established relationship between the executive and legislative departments with consequences that cannot be accurately foreseen and appraised."

Close analysis makes this at once apparent. If the cabinet is to sit in Congress, the president must choose its members from those who are likely to be influential with it. This at once narrows his choice. It makes him think of the men who already have some standing in its eyes, and some direct knowledge of its complicated procedure. But this means putting a premium on the experienced members of either house as cabinet material. It means, further, that the more successful they are upon the floor of Congress, the more independent they are likely to be vis-à-vis the president. They will develop a status of their own as they become known as the men who are able to make Congress take their views about the bills they promote. They are likely, in fact, to become rivals of the president himself for influence with Congress. The problem, in this situation, of maintaining cabinet unity would necessarily become a difficult matter. Congress

[14] *American National Government* (1931), p. 316.

might easily tend to weaken the administration by playing off the cabinet, or some part of it, against the president and some other part. The loyalty of the cabinet officer would be divided. Is he, for example, to support the president on a scheme like the Court plan, and thereby to weaken his standing with Congress; or is he discreetly to make known his dislike for the plan in the hope that he may thereby win approval for some bill in which he is interested?

The president's problem of changing his cabinet would, moreover, be immensely intensified. Is he to keep an officer about whose full loyalty he is dubious, but whose influence on Congress is clearly great? Can he prevent such an officer's so nearly rivaling his own authority as to make his own position exceptionally difficult? Would not the position of a president like Lincoln, whose hold on his own colleagues was small when he assumed power, become virtually untenable if Congress were in a position to play them off against him? Is there not, indeed, the danger of a powerful cabal of cabinet officers' becoming the effective mediator between the president and Congress with a vital shift, as a consequence, in the present delicate balance of power? Would it not, further, be likely that a tendency would rapidly develop for any cabinet officer who became outstandingly influential with Congress to become the rival of the president himself, and, where the latter was weak, in actual fact his master?

More than even this is, I think, involved. There would develop the tendency for the president to

choose his cabinet from Congress in order to maximize his influence with it, and thus to transfer the
leadership of his party there to a room, so to say, of
which he only had the key. There would be a tendency for cabinet officers to use their relation with
Congress as a platform from which to reach the presidency, with all the difficulties of colleagueship of this
position, and more, that Polk emphasized. It is difficult, moreover, not to feel that, in these circumstances,
the advice of the cabinet member upon questions of
patronage would be given under conditions altogether
different from and inferior to those upon which they
now depend. The danger of trading posts for measures is already profound enough in the American system; it is difficult not to feel that it would be greatly
intensified if a cabinet officer were independent of
the president in his power to influence Congress. The
coherence that is now given to administrative action
by the supremacy of the president might easily be
jeopardized by this aspect alone.

The Pendleton scheme suggested that cabinet members should have access to debates upon the floor of
the House. But in fact, the main business of Congress
is performed in secret committees to which the public has no access. No cabinet officer could adequately
look after his measures unless he penetrated the committee rooms also. But were he to do so, the control
over him of the president would be still further diminished; and the relation between him and Congress
would rival in closeness that with the executive of
which the president is the head. This seems scarcely

desirable in a system where there is no collective cabinet responsibility, and where the unity of the executive structure is supplied by presidential control. In
these circumstances, no cabinet member can be transformed into an automaton who merely reflects the
presidential will. For first, in such a transformation as
this innovation portends, he would have been chosen
just precisely because he is not an automaton; and
second, to the degree that he seeks to act like one, he
defeats the whole object of the innovation.

There are two further difficulties in the scheme,
moreover, to which adequate attention has hardly been
given in discussion of it. It raises most delicate and
complicated questions of the relation between the cabinet officer, as a quasi-member of Congress, and the
senator or congressman who is in charge of the bill
in which he is interested. By whom is the concession
to be made to a proposed amendment? How will chair-
manships be arranged so as to secure a proper harmony in congressional proceedings between the cabinet officer and the chairman of his committee? On a
bill, for example, like that of President Roosevelt's
Court plan, the position of the attorney-general
would be well-nigh intolerable unless he were at one
with the chairman of the Judiciary Committee. The
fact is that, on the present system, where the chairmen of the important committees of both houses form
a kind of quasi-executive within the two branches of
the legislature, the position of cabinet officers would
be impossible at every point where they disagreed
with that quasi-executive. Either they would be

tempted into a position of continuous inferiority for the sake of agreement, in which difficult questions of loyalty to the president would be involved; or they would differ openly with the official chairmen of the legislative committees, in which case, they would greatly add, by that difference, to the burden the president had to carry.

Nor is this all. The Pendleton scheme seems to assume that each cabinet officer is to sit in Congress merely in relation to his own department. But the categories of government are far from being as simple as this view would make them appear. The range of modern legislation makes the secretary of the treasury as ubiquitously relevant as the chancellor of the exchequer in relation to most government proposals. The interrelations of modern problems of defense make half the issues which arise matters of co-ordination to which the secretary of the treasury, the secretary of war, and the secretary of the navy are all relevant. On foreign affairs, every vital matter is at least a joint operation between the president and the secretary of state; the latter could hardly offer an opinion in Congress save as he affirmed that outlook for which he had prior approval from the president; and in matters of supreme importance it is the president only whose attitude it is vital for Congress to know. There, as the Wilson administration makes clear, he supersedes the secretary of state far more emphatically than, in an analogous situation, the prime minister of England supersedes (he rather supplements) the foreign secretary. Similar difficulties

[104]

arise as between the Departments of Commerce and
Labor; and the Department of Justice, especially in
the context of prosecutions such as those under the
Sherman Act, has a vital relation to many other departments. It is, in fact, difficult to see how any cabinet officer except the postmaster-general could be
confined within any rigidly defined domain. In the
result, most cabinet officers would—whatever the system started as—be bound to develop roving commissions of general relevance not very different from the
part that a cabinet minister plays in the British House
of Commons.

It must, moreover, be remembered that in the
American system the initiative in legislation does not
lie, as with Great Britain, for effective purposes in the
government only. No doubt a special pre-eminence attaches to bills which have, so to say, the imprimatur of
the president. But the source of a good deal of important legislative action lies in the hands of individual
senators and congressmen; in this respect it is only
necessary to remember how much has been done,
often despite the administration, by men like the late
Senator La Follette and by Senator Norris. It would
be far from easy to adjust the delicate relations which
would arise from this dual relationship, not least if
the president were in a minority in Congress. And if
members of the cabinet were admitted only to the
floor of both houses, they would, for the most part,
miss the chance of participation in the pivotal consideration of bills; while, if they were permitted their

full share in the committee processes, the duality of leadership would create almost insoluble problems.

The Pendleton scheme, in short, does not meet the real problems created by the presidential system. The facts of American life have concentrated literally enormous power in the hands of the president; and it is no doubt true that the exercise of this power produces, above all in a second term, grave congressional doubts of the wisdom of its extent. At some time in the tenure of a president with a majority, the accusation of autocracy is almost bound to arise. But the real outcome of the Pendleton scheme, or any variant upon it, would be, I think, to transfer the essential features of presidential leadership to the cabinet. Its operations in Congress would be bound, sooner or later, to become the axis upon which the authority of the administration turned. I believe, indeed, that properly to perform its function in Congress the cabinet would be bound to try and discover the terms upon which it could become a unity; a unity, be it noted, not only against the Congress, but against the president also. The latter would be compelled to spend a good deal of his energy in maintaining his authority against colleagues who would have developed an interest and prestige at least parallel to his own, and, conceivably, different from it. None of them could fail to be aware that outstanding success in the handling of Congress was the highroad to the kind of reputation out of which a presidential nomination could be secured. Some of them, at least, would be bound to play for that nomination; and the problem, in those circumstances, of maintaining presidential supremacy would be at every point delicate and complicated.

The real result, in a word, of the adoption of such a scheme as Senator Pendleton proposed would be very rapidly to transform the president into a person more akin to the president of the French Republic than to that of the United States. He could not avoid the certainty that his colleagues who became pivotal in Congress would soon become indispensable to him. He could hardly avoid the concentration of public attention upon their activities in Congress rather than upon his relations with it. He would have to watch those activities with a jealous eye lest they impinge upon the sphere of influence that is at present his own. The man among them who became the congressional leader of the cabinet would soon become a figure akin in character and influence to the prime minister; the president would be dependent upon him for every legislative move in the fulfilment of his program. Indeed, I think it not unlikely that the president would become rather the adviser than the master of the man to whom Congress looked for the formulation and defense of the presidential program; he would be moved to second place. He would find it difficult to resist the pressure of a cabinet officer who was influential with Congress; he might well jeopardize his own position if he asked for his resignation. A hostile Congress might even play off the cabinet, or some section of it, against him.

On any showing, this is to say, the Pendleton

scheme would wholly alter the balance of forces history has evolved in the American system of government. I do not say that it would necessarily alter them for the worse; any such estimate depends upon a comparison between the presidential and parliamentary systems that is here out of place. All I am concerned to argue is that latent in the scheme is a revolution in the historical conception of the presidency. As it now operates, the nation looks to the president for executive leadership, and, in the long run, circumstances make it difficult for that leadership to be found elsewhere. Such a scheme as Pendleton's inherently threatens that authority. While it separates him from his cabinet, on the one hand, it builds a bridge between the cabinet and Congress, on the other; and the president cannot walk across that bridge. It gives the cabinet an interest against him, not only with the legislature, but also with the party. A generation which has seen the vice-president of the United States use his influence in Congress to intrigue against the president should have no difficulty in seeing what his position might become if to his influence were joined that of any considerable part of the cabinet. At present, at any rate, when the president and Congress are at odds, the former's power of direct appeal to the nation makes the issue between them a clear one upon which public opinion can make up its mind. A cabinet that moved toward independence of him would make such a clarity of choice a difficult matter. It would, almost necessarily, divert a good deal of attention away from the case the president has to make. It would offer the possibility of great rewards to those about him who were prepared to risk the penalties of disloyalty to him. Anyone who reflects upon the position that might have arisen if Stanton had been able to utilize Congress as a platform against Andrew Johnson can see the potentialities that are latent in this change.

It may be, as I have said, that it should be attempted; for it may well be that the burden which the present situation imposes upon the president is greater than any statesman, above all in a democratic community, should be asked to bear. But the change should not be attempted without a full knowledge that it will profoundly alter the historic contours of the presidential system. It may not, in the first instance, transform it on the lines of the parliamentary system; it is bound, I have argued, in the long run to move it toward those lines. It cannot do so, on all experience, without two results. It must first depreciate the position of the man who cannot directly influence the congressional process; those, to use my earlier metaphor, are bound to be nearer to it who cross the bridge than those who stay on the other side. And if men are sought who can influence Congress, men are bound to be sought by whom Congress is prepared to be influenced. That does not only mean the device of a different kind of cabinet officer from those of the past. It means also, in the long run, men who realize that the way to influence a legislative assembly is to be responsive to its will; and that is the first step toward responsibility to its wishes. Fundamentally, this is to alter the whole balance of the American Constitution. It is to make it desirable to build a cabinet which can sway Congress. That makes the main lever of executive authority resident in the cabinet rather than in the president. While this may be a better scheme than the present one, its possible merits cannot conceal the fact that it is a constitutional revolution of the first magnitude. It is to dig into the foundations of the state; and that, as Edmund Burke insisted, is always a dangerous adventure.

III

THE PRESIDENT AND CONGRESS

I

UNDER all normal circumstances, it is difficult not to feel that the president of the United States must envy the legislative position of a British prime minister. The latter is the head of an assured parliamentary majority; unless he has made a grave blunder, it is nowadays the electorate, and not Parliament, which destroys his measures. He and his cabinet have the effective initiative in all legislation, above all in finance; and they do not find it necessary, save on the rarest occasions, to yield to sectional pressure. The prime minister has no interest he need consult in the making of appointments; there is unlikely to be serious question even about those of which there are grave doubts among his followers. He takes the fundamental part in the definition of all issues. While he remains prime minister, he is the unquestioned master of his party machine. He is, moreover, the master of the House of Commons through his power over its dissolution; he decides when the moment is propitious for an election. He is unlikely to retire from the leadership of his party except at his own discretion; and the fact that he will lead it to the polls means, normally, the nearer the approach of a general election, the more complete will be his power over his party. No doubt, over a period, the condition of his hold is that he shall be successful; but, granted that he can lead it to victory once in a decade, he has little reason to fear the emergence of a rival.[1]

At almost every point in the pattern British practice has traced, there is a wide divergence from the presidential situation. The president is never the master of Congress, except in relatively brief intervals of emergency. He does not know that it will accept his principles of action; as Polk insisted,[2] and as Franklin Roosevelt has learned, even a great majority in both houses is no guarantee of his control. He may not even have a nominal majority, and, in that event, he can be sure that the main purpose of Congress will be to discredit his administration. He cannot exercise over either house the threat of dissolution; whether he will or no, its elections are determined by a time-table over which he has no say. He may influence the choice of congressional leaders but he cannot determine them; all the prestige of Franklin Roosevelt only enabled Senator Barkley to succeed Senator Robinson by a single vote. There is no continuous power to secure disciplined voting; and Mr. Coolidge found that a small number of recalcitrant legislators may be fatal to his plans. Neither he nor his cabinet directly participate in the work of Congress; they are dependent upon legislators whose own view of the wise course

---

[1] Cf. my *Parliamentary Government in England* (1938), pp. 239-241.
[2] *Op. cit.*, p. 186.

to follow is not less important than theirs. He can, no doubt, exercise some discipline over rebels in his own party; but the attempted "purge" of 1938 makes it clear that this authority reaches but a little way. He may initiate legislation; and he can be sure that a respectful attention will be given to his proposals. But he will always find that there are, in either house, perhaps half a dozen men with independent authority to promote legislation independently of him. He can be sure, too, that whatever his convenience, either house, or both houses, will spend a considerable part of their energies investigating his administration; and unlike the British prime minister, he will be largely unable to determine to his own advantage the composition of the investigating committees. While he is nominally the head of his party, and, while in office, the chief factor in the operation of its machine, the knowledge that in eight years at most he will have ceased to be president profoundly limits his power to determine the uses to which it shall be put.

To grasp the difference between the two systems, it is essential to bear certain points in mind. The House of Commons is only formally a legislative assembly; in this context its real business is to act as the cabinet's organ of registration. It may secure minor amendments; it may even, on rare occasions, secure the withdrawal of a proposal. But, fundamentally, legislation is shaped in Whitehall, and not in Westminster. With Congress, this is not the case. Legislation is the main business of both houses. They do not act under the instructions of the president; they may co-operate with him if they feel so inclined. But they are at every point, save in periods of grave crisis, equal partners with him, and in the event of difference they, rather than he, are likely to have their way. He has, of course, the right of veto; but that is rather a reserve weapon of last instance than one of habitual use. It is, indeed, true to say that the influential members of Congress have, in their legislative capacity, more power than any private members of any other legislative assembly in the world.

This is the case for a number of reasons. It is inherent, in the first place, in the division of powers; the founders of the Constitution did not intend the president to have authority to do more than indicate a general direction; particularity was assumed to be the proper business of a legislature. It is the case, secondly, because Congress is the legislature of a continent rather than of a country in the European sense of the word. A member of Congress is expected, by reason of the vast size of the United States, to think in terms of sectional not less than national interests. He has to think about the effect of the measures to be considered upon the character of the particular area for which he sits; and what he believes (sometimes wrongly) to be its will, may not infrequently cut across the will of the administration. A member of the House of Representatives must be constantly aware that every two years he will be judged by his constituents; and this makes him far more responsive to his judgment of what will please them than he is likely to be to what will satisfy the president. For him, normally, the local issue and its repercussions are likely to seem far more acute than the national, not least if the outcome of the next primary is at all seriously in dispute. A congress-man, moreover, whose fate may depend upon the judgment of a local boss (in his turn, perhaps, the crea-ture of an important public utility corporation) is likely to feel that the advice of the boss is far more relevant to his future than that of the president. The members of Congress from the silver-producing states would not lightly go back to their constituencies and explain that, in the national interest, they saw no alter-native but to accept the views of Wall Street upon the gold standard; and a president who sought to en-force stringent legislation against lynching would find that he encountered a definitely particularistic view from Southern congressmen and senators. There is a real sense in which all but a handful of especially eminent senators, whose return to the Senate has be-come almost a tradition, may be regarded as members of "special areas," for whose interests they must press, and to whose peculiarities they must yield, whatever be the outlook of the president and the party.

It is important, thirdly, that the Congress has an in-terest separate from that of the president. No doubt the common tie of party binds them together; but it is vital to realize that it never binds them into a unity. From the first presidency of Washington onward, Congress has made its will to independence apparent; and only war, or an emergency like that of March, 1933, has secured the transcendence of that will. Partly, it is a matter of pride; the Congress must show that it takes its orders from none but itself. Partly, it is the realization that the life of the administration does not depend on its having its own way. Partly, no doubt, the individual congressman feels that he is more genuinely a person by enforcing his right to assert himself. For there is always a real fear in Congress of being overshadowed by the president. To enforce alterations is to draw attention to itself, to secure understanding that he is not the unqualified master of the nation. There can be no doubt that, in its own eyes, Congress establishes its prestige when it either refuses to let the president have his own way, or compels him to compromise with it. Unlike the House of Commons with the prime minister, it can do so without penalty. So far as possible, therefore, it likes to make every measure submitted to it a little different from the form in which it is received. That enhances its stature in its own eyes, and, on occasion, it enhances its stature in the eyes of the electorate. There is always a pleasure in informing the head of the nation that there are limits to his power.

The system, I think, makes both for incoherency and irresponsibility, not least in the realm of finance. It makes for the first because, whatever the effort the president may make, the legislation of any given Congress is not unified; it does not derive from a single mind. Some measures are directly presidential in principle; though it will be rare for them to have the exact form the president may wish to give them. Others may come from the will of an important senator who can count on the backing of his colleagues; others, again, may derive from a sectional group, irrespective of party, who demand them as the price of supporting other measures. Particularly in finance, where the American system forbids any real unity of control either in ways and means or in appropriation, the outlook of a powerful chairman may make a great difference to the measures Congress will pass; and to this the budgetary system introduced nearly twenty years ago has made little difference. It is perhaps an exaggeration to say that the opinion of the chairman of the Senate Committee on Interstate Commerce will, on a big railroad question, count as much as the opinion of the president; but it is not, I think, an exaggeration to say that, where they differ, the Senate will compel the president to make sufficient of a compromise with its chairman to show that the senator has not been defeated by the presidential will. There is certainly no appropriations act which does not spend literally millions of dollars upon objectives the president does not approve and is compelled to accept as the price for securing other objectives about which he feels keenly.

The system makes also for irresponsibility. Because the influences which go to make legislation are so diverse, there can be no clear allocation of blame. Each house of Congress can proceed upon its own lines; only too often, they evolve a compromise which does not satisfy either, and is not the legislation which the president intended. There are, too, measures of considerable importance, like that, for instance, relating to the soldiers' bonus, which Congress will pass in defiance of the presidential veto simply because it dare not risk the unpopularity a powerful lobby like the American Legion may seek to organize against it. It will yield to sudden gusts of ignorant temper. The Reorganization Bill of 1938, for example, (which it passed in substantially similar form in 1939) was defeated largely as the result of indefensible propaganda which represented it, quite inaccurately, as a vast enlargement of presidential power. If it be true that the British member of Parliament obeys too rigidly the crack of his party whip, it is still more true that the member of Congress is prone to an anarchism about the substance of measures for which there is no defense. The "pork barrel" legislation of the last century is the measure of this anarchism. Without regard to the problems the president confronts, it has been built upon an interchange of sectional interests for which, quite unjustifiably, the taxpayer has been called upon to pay. Much the same is true of pensions; much the same is true of the tariff; much the same is true of agricultural measures like the McNary-Haughen bill. The separation of powers erodes responsibility by dividing it; and the result is not only an immense increase of the costs of government.

It is also a temptation to a weak president to evade the responsibility of leadership. This was true, very notably, of men like Buchanan and Harding and Coolidge. They do not tackle the problems they ought to tackle; they accept measures they think mistaken both in principle and in detail because they are afraid to have trouble with Congress. The system not only results in a prenatal control of legislation upon subjects either difficult or unpopular. It offers an opportunity to powerful lobbies to multiply the area in which prenatal control operates with a weak president by playing on his fears. No one can read the history of the attempts to deal with the slavery question without seeing that this is the case. No one, either, can read the painful effort of Edward Moseley to secure essential legislation for railroad safety[3] without seeing how a lobby as powerful as that of the railroads can persuade both president and Congress to neglect an obvious duty. Even a strong president, like Franklin Roosevelt, is driven to postpone issues which he believes to be urgent by the fact that one or other of the lobbies at Washington may dissipate party coherency through the local influences it can bring to bear. With a weak president, this leads to the making of concessions which he knows to be indefensible. And even if the pressure of public opinion, as with the trusts, compels Congress, under presidential impulse, to action, the positive execution of the measure concerned will halt. That has certainly been the case with the Sherman Act. Even a president as positive as Theodore Roosevelt engaged largely in shadow-boxing with the great corporations for fear of the influence they might bring to bear at the other end of Pennsylvania Avenue.

The system, further, puts a premium on sectionalism. It is difficult, anyhow, to draw any clear line be-

[3] See the history of his achievement admirably related in James Morgan's biography of him.

tween the major American parties; and the degree to which they hold the field is shown by the fact that, with but five exceptions since 1860, the Republican and Democratic parties have polled, between them, over 90 per cent of the votes in presidential elections. It is, however, true to say that with the possible exception of some of the major measures since 1933, there is no measure that has been put upon the statute-book by one party which could not have been put there by another. The parties gain their majorities by the appeal they make to sectional interests;[4] and individual members take leave to think in sectional rather than in party terms. There is, in fact, more in common between a Democrat like Senator Wheeler of Montana and a Republican like the late Senator Borah of Idaho, than there is between Senator Glass, the Democratic senator from Virginia, and Mr. Wheeler, or between Senator Hastings of Delaware, a conservative Republican, and a Senator Borah. The votes of each are determined by considerations which transcend party lines in a way hardly understood in Great Britain; and the presidential problem of securing coherency is greatly aggravated as a consequence. In legislation regulating hours and wages in commodities of interstate commerce, for instance, a Democratic senator or congressman from Massachusetts is bound to think less of the party line than of the effect on his constituency of so voting as to offer the prospect of being criticized in Massachusetts because he has sacri-

[4] See this well worked out by Professor A. N. Holcomb in E. B. Logan, *The American Political Scene* (1938), pp. 1-52, 289-304.

ficed its industrial interests to the lower standard of life which prevails in the South. A progressive-minded Southerner like Mr. Maury Maverick of Texas is pretty certain to pay by defeat for insisting that southern industry ought not, in matters of industrial legislation, to be parasitic upon its low standard of life. *Mutatis mutandis*, this is true of a large part of the field of social and economic action.

All this is to say that it tempts the Congress to avoid unity of outlook except under immense pressure from the White House. It follows the presidential lead instinctively only when it would be fatal for it not to follow that lead. Fatality depends on three things. There may be external war, as in 1898 and 1917; there may be grave internal emergency, as in 1933; or there may be a public opinion so widespread in favor of the presidential policy that the Congress finds it unwise to follow its own bent. But the result is the clear one—the mechanism of which I shall discuss later—that the means a president must use to secure the unity he requires are all quite different from anything the founders could have imagined. They built a weak executive, they divided the sources of legislative power, because at the time they did their work the mental climate of the time called for that attitude. It is even possible to argue that it was an intelligible outlook down to some such period as the Civil War. Since then, and in increasing degree, it has been a hindrance, and not a help, to the proper performance of the president's duties. And this conclusion is not vitiated by the fact that some presidents—Mr.

Coolidge, for example—had rarely any idea in the situation they confronted of what those duties were.

The situation is difficult enough when the president's party is in a majority in both houses. Then, at least, the party interest in re-election enables him to use the pressures at his disposal to maintain some measure of effective power. But if he loses that majority, as was evident in the administration of Hayes and in the last years of Wilson's presidency, he is in a hopeless position. In those circumstances the Congress naturally feels that it has nothing to gain by co-operating with him; and its term is passed in a mutual evasion of responsibility which has rarely any point save playing for advantage at the next presidential election. Measures may well be passed, even with a presidential majority, to which the president himself has the strongest possible objection; and, if his veto is inoperative, he is compelled—the supreme folly in administration—to execute policies of which he disapproves. A good example of this habit was the decision of Congress in 1939 to discontinue the cultural experiments made under the Works Progress Administration. All observers of them who had any serious acquaintance with their achievement were aware that they represented an epoch in the history of the relation between government and the arts. They were sacrificed because the opposition to the president had determined to make "economy" an issue of the campaign of 1940; and, though the sum involved was small, his nominal supporters took the view that the enemy could not be allowed to put—what they would in any case put—the need for economy before the electorate as an issue. The cultural experiment was therefore abandoned, despite the pressure of the president. But he was still left with the important administrative issue of how to find effective means of relief for those who would be rendered unemployed by reason of their abandonment.

2

This leads to one conclusion which is of great importance to the proper understanding of the relation between Congress and the president. Its own instinctive and inherent tendency is, under all circumstances, to be anti-presidential. It may respect him; it may even fear him; it may give him a general if spasmodic support. But it is always looking for occasions to differ from him, and it never feels so really comfortable as when it has found such an occasion for difference. In doing so, it has the sense that it is affirming its own essence. It is more truly itself because it is exalting its own prestige. Some members, no doubt, act in this way because to fight the president is the highroad to notoriety. Others, the late Senator Borah, for example, are constitutionally uncomfortable if they support any president while he is in office. In the Senate, especially, a good deal of truth lies in the remark of President Coolidge that most senators think they ought to be president, and that, in any case, they know more than he does. In the Senate, again, something is due to the fact that the chairman of an important committee is likely to have been there for many years. He has become a specialist in his allotted field. He has seen presidents and cabinet officers come and go; it is only human, perhaps, for him to think, first, that his own view of what should be done is better than their view, and, second, that to enhance his own prestige it is important for him to change any presidential measure sufficiently to leave his own mark upon it. Mark Hanna and Roscoe Conkling are perhaps extreme instances of men who sought to move their colleagues to take the view, in the one case privately, in the other by public dispute, that the credit of their institution depended upon keeping the president in its leading strings.

The history of Congress, and especially of the Senate, might well from one angle be summarized as a continuous effort to make the president its creature; of the Senate, in particular, because its relation to the appointing power and to foreign relations, in addition to the fact that the career of the average senator will normally outlast that of several presidents, give it a special advantage in seeking to enforce its view. No one can read such documents as the diaries of John Quincy Adams, of Polk, of Gideon Welles, or the autobiographies of senators like Blaine and Hoar of Massachusetts without seeing that this is the case. The administration of President Grant was, no doubt, a particularly flagrant example of a Congress without any real sense of obligation; but it is notable that even from a senator with cabinet experience it evoked no blame. "The executive department of a republic like ours," wrote John Sherman, "should be subordinate to the legislative department. The president should obey and enforce the laws, leaving to the people the duty of correcting any errors committed by their representatives in Congress."[5] "The most eminent senators," wrote Hoar, then a congressman, of this period, "would have received as a personal affront a private message from the White House expressing a desire that they should adopt any course in the discharge of their legislative duties that they did not approve. If they visited the White House, it was to give, not to receive, advice. Any little company or coterie who had undertaken to arrange public policies with the president and to report to their associates what the president thought would have rapidly come to grief. . . . Each of these stars kept his own orbit and shone in his sphere, within which he tolerated no intrusion from the president or from anybody else."[6]

No doubt the aftermath of the Civil War was an exceptional period; but for at least the fifteen years succeeding it, the thesis of the Senate was that presidents should run in leading strings that it would control. Even the cabinet of Hayes was not confirmed until a storm of popular disapproval had arisen.[7] The actions of the Senate in those years are inexplicable except upon the assumption that it was determined to make the president no more than its creature. Even when its claims had to be diminished under the force

[5] *Recollections of Forty Years in the House, Senate and Cabinet* (1895), p. 447.
[6] *Autobiography* (1903), II, 46.
[7] *Diary of R. B. Hayes* (ed. Williams, 1922), entries for March, 1877.

of public opinion, they remained as a threat to become operative at the first opportunity. It assumed the right to supervise in itemized detail the conduct of every executive agency it had brought into being. It believed that it was its duty to investigate each executive action, and, as in the classic case of Cleveland's nomination of Burnett to the office of district attorney in Alabama, to see all confidential papers in connection with the administrative process.[8] The impression produced on a careful observer of this period is worth noting. Congress, wrote Woodrow Wilson,[9] "does not domineer over the president himself, but it makes the secretaries its humble servants. Not that it would hesitate, upon occasion, to deal directly with the chief magistrate himself; but it has few calls to do so, because our latter-day presidents live by proxy; they are executives in theory, but the secretaries are executives in fact." Until at any rate the late eighties of the last century it is not unfair to accept Wilson's description of the president as, in the eyes of Congress, "merely the executor of the sovereign legislative will."[10] Only a few years later Lord Bryce was recording the view that "the president's wishes conveyed in a message have not necessarily any more effect on Congress than an article in a prominent party newspaper . . . and, in fact, the suggestions which he makes, year after year, are usually neglected, even when his party has a

[8] Cleveland, *Presidential Problems* (1904), pp. 46 f.

[9] *Congressional Government* (1885), p. 45.

[10] Cf. his illuminating article, "The Presidency in 1879" in the *International Review*, VI, 46.

majority in both houses, or when the subject lies outside party lines."[11]

From Grant to the election of McKinley the center of effective power was in Congress, and save for an occasional revolt most of the presidents seemed, at least publicly, content that it should be so. The picture of what, in an eminent Republican's eyes, they ought to seek to be, was drawn for Benjamin Harrison by John Sherman. "The president," he wrote,[12] "should have no policy distinct from that of his party, and this is better represented in Congress than in the executive." Hayes and Cleveland may have had their moments of challenge, but even the fact that they were supported in them by public opinion did not lead them to attempt any continuity of leadership. It was not until McKinley arrived at the White House that the balance began to swing in the presidential direction. Partly, no doubt, this was due to the fact that the Spanish-American War forced upon him, as war forced upon the Whig Lincoln, a direction he could hardly avoid; partly, too, his long period in the House of Representatives gave him a skill in congressional maneuver that his predecessors from Grant onward had lacked. Senator Hoar, indeed, after a generation's experience, expressed the view that no president, save possibly Jackson, had exercised the influence over the Senate that McKinley did.[13] Perhaps this was because the entrance of America into international politics as

[11] *American Commonwealth* (1908), I, 230.
[12] *Op. cit.*, p. 1032.
[13] *Op. cit.*, II, 47.

a world power gave him, consciously to himself, a new status; there is significance in his remark that "I can no longer be called the president of a party; I am now the president of the whole people."[14]

The leadership that McKinley exercised in an unostentatious way was exercised by Theodore Roosevelt with a determined aggressiveness that had been unknown since Jackson. He had, as he has himself told us, a theory of the presidential power which placed its exponent in the forefront of the political stage. "The executive power," he wrote,[15] "was limited only by specific instructions and prohibitions appearing in the Constitution, or imposed by Congress under its constitutional powers. My view was that every executive officer, and above all every executive officer in a high position, was a steward of all the people bound actively and affirmatively to do all he could for the people. . . . I did not usurp power, but I did greatly broaden the use of executive power." That was not an unfair description of his practice. It ought to be added that much of its success was due to his collaboration with Speaker Cannon,[16] that in the last years of his presidency there was a visible and significant decline in the force of his leadership, and that his successor, William Howard Taft, whom he virtually nominated, went back to a view of the presidential office more akin to that of Cleveland than to that of Roosevelt.[17] Woodrow Wilson, in his turn, re-

[14] Olcott, *Life of William McKinley* (1916), II, 296.
[15] *Autobiography* (1913), p. 389.
[16] L. W. Bushey, *Uncle Joe Cannon* (1927), p. 219.
[17] *Our Chief Magistrate* (1916), pp. 139-142.

newed and extended the Roosevelt conception. It was not merely that he was the first president since Washington personally to place his program before Congress. Even before he took office he had revolted against the notion that he was the instrument of congressional purposes. "The president is at liberty," he wrote in 1906,[18] "both in law and in conscience to be as big a man as he can. His capacity will set the limit." He is entitled to seek the leadership of the nation because, if he succeeds, it is because "the president has the nation behind him and Congress has not. . . . The Constitution explicitly authorizes the President to recommend to Congress 'such measures as he shall deem necessary and expedient,' and it is not necessary to the integrity of even the literary theory of the Constitution to insist that recommendations shall be merely perfunctory. . . . The Constitution bids him speak, and times of stress must more and more thrust upon him the attitude of originator of policies."[19]

Those last words are significant, and they must be read, I think, in terms of the development he gave them just after his election and before he took office. "The president," he wrote,[20] "is expected by the nation to be the leader of his party, as well as the chief executive officer of the government, and the country will take no excuses from him. He must play the part, and play it successfully, or lose the country's confidence. He must be prime minister, as much con-

[18] *Constitutional Government in the United States* (1907), p. 69.
[19] *Ibid.*, pp. 70-73.
[20] Letter to A. Mitchell Palmer in H. J. Ford, *Woodrow Wilson* (1916), where it is printed as an appendix.

cerned with the guidance of legislation as with the just and orderly execution of law, and he is the spokesman of the nation in everything, even the most momentous and delicate dealings of the government in foreign affairs." The theory of Woodrow Wilson corresponded closely to his practice. In the first two years of his administration, Congress was driven to pass an important series of domestic measures of which he was himself the chief architect. With the coming of war, he assumed the headship of the nation to a degree, and with powers, beyond any that Lincoln received. It is significant that he refused to accept a cabinet of national concentration, and that he stopped the movement which sought to repeat the Lincolnian precedent by associating with him a committee of both houses of Congress to assist him in the conduct of the war. Until the eve of the armistice, he was the unquestioned master of the nation. "Senators of sovereign states and leaders of parties," writes one commentator,[21] "grovelled in their marble corridors, so terrified were they of public opinion."

But Wilson pushed public opinion too far. With the coming of peace, the idea of the almost personal sovereignty he had exercised aroused discontent everywhere; and his opponents won a majority in the Congress of 1918. Thenceforward, he was impotent; and until 1932 the pendulum swung back to a stage where the effective leadership was in Congress and not in the president. In part, at least, this was due to the presidents themselves. Both Harding and Coolidge

[21] G. R. Brown, *The Leadership of Congress* (1922), p. 187.

were mediocrities. The first had pledged himself, before election, to a "revival of party government as distinguished from personal government," by which he meant that he would follow Congress and not lead it; and, indeed, his nomination was mainly due to the realization of the chiefs of the Republican party that he was the type of man who would accept guidance. The treatment of his first budget in Congress, of which he expressed the hope that Congress would make no substantial changes, is typical of the treatment he received. The Committee on Appropriations examined the estimates of his Bureau of the Budget so minutely that the printed testimony of their examination occupies over twenty thousand pages of print; and they reduced them by over three hundred million dollars.[22] Mr. Coolidge was hardly in better case. There were, in fact, few subjects upon which he had any ideas, and his general approach to politics was built upon the assumption that there was, in any circumstances, too much legislation. He did not, therefore, try to give any lead. "I have never felt," he wrote,[23] "that it was my duty to attempt to coerce senators or representatives, or to take reprisals. The people sent them to Washington. I felt I had discharged my duty when I had done the best I could with them. In this way I avoided almost entirely a personal opposition, which I think was of more value to the country than to attempt to prevail through arousing personal fear." The period, in fact, from

[22] *Congressional Record* (67th Congress, 2nd Sess.), p. 11, 665.
[23] *Autobiography* (1929), p. 232.

1921 to 1929 was the era of conscious abdication from power on the part of the president. Neither really appealed to the country for support against Congress, because neither had any policy for which to appeal. Each was content to give his party a free run of power; and each assumed that the idea of the free run for the party meant the almost unfettered dominance of Congress. Congress, of course, was content to accept this view.

The problem of the Hoover administration was a different one. Harding and Coolidge were mediocre hack politicians whose main recommendation to their colleagues was their very mediocrity. Mr. Hoover, with little political experience, came to office as an expert administrator, more or less in specific contrast to his predecessors. He encountered an emergency hardly less great than the war itself; yet he seemed entirely unable to assume the leadership of Congress in that emergency. What is the reason? Partly, no doubt, it derives from his acceptance of a rigorous concept of the separation of powers. "The weakening of the legislative arm," he wrote in 1934,[24] "[leads] to encroachment by the executive upon the legislative and judicial functions, and inevitably that encroachment is upon individual liberty. If we examine the fate of wrecked republics over the world we shall find first a weakening of the legislative arm." Something of this affirmation is, of course, a direct criticism of the policy pursued by his successor, Franklin D. Roosevelt. But it is also explicit in his actual relations

[24] *The Challenge to Liberty* (1934), pp. 125-126.

with Congress. Tariffs and farm relief, he said shortly after taking office, are matters for Congress to determine; his duty was merely to draw attention to them.[25] Though he cordially disapproved of the Hawley-Smoot tariff, he refused to use his influence against it, on the ground that he could not know enough of its details to recommend specific alterations of them. He was deeply unpopular in Washington; and this seems to have bred a self-distrust in him which made him shrink from the emphasis of leadership.[26] Perhaps, also, the depth of his attachment to a laissez faire philosophy inhibited him from recommending that positive action which would have meant government interference with matters he conceived as the concern of business men only. While he was in office, at any rate, it was in Congress and not in him that the direction of affairs was centralized. It is not, I think, unfair to suggest that it was the public consciousness of the fact that he did not lead in the face of the great depression which was largely responsible for his defeat in the election of 1932.

Though the last six years are still living events, it happens that, in the context of this discussion, we are better informed about them than about any of the three previous administrations. The publication by President Roosevelt of his papers[27] makes available not only his public addresses, but also his private conferences with the press, and his annotations upon the

[25] Cf. the criticism in the *New Republic*, Vol. 58, p. 184.
[26] *New Republic*, June 4, 1930.
[27] *The Public Papers and Addresses of Franklin D. Roosevelt* (1938), 5 vols.

whole. It is hardly too much to say that these give us an insight into the working of the presidency such as we have not had since the diaries of John Quincy Adams and of Polk. From our angle, what they represent is a revival and extension of the theory of the presidency of which Theodore Roosevelt and Woodrow Wilson were the exponents. The drive to action comes from the White House. Franklin Roosevelt's conception of his office is intensely positive. Whether in foreign policy or in domestic affairs, the material Congress is made to consider is material for which he demands consideration. I shall discuss later the methods by which he has enforced consideration. Here it is sufficient to say that he has throughout chosen to lead, and has compelled Congress to follow.

But what is significant in the experience of Franklin Roosevelt is not merely the extent and the intensity of the lead he has given; what is significant also is the growth and dissent from the fact of this leadership in Congress. In the first "hundred days," the emergency was so great that he secured from Congress everything for which he asked. It responded without limit to the challenge he uttered. "In the event," he told it,[28] "that the Congress shall fail to take these courses, and in the event that the national emergency is still critical, I shall not evade the clear course of duty that will then confront me. I shall ask the Congress for the one remaining instrument to meet the crisis—broad executive power to wage a war against the emergency as great as the power that would be given to me if we

[28] *Public Papers* (1938), II, 15.

[134]

were in fact invaded by a foreign foe." The remark of the Republican leader in the House of Representatives in the debate on the emergency banking bill best expresses the attitude of Congress to this challenge. "The house," he said,[29] "is burning down, and the President of the United States says this is the way to put out the fire." It may be doubted whether, even during the World War, there had been so complete an acceptance of presidential leadership as in those hundred days.

In the president's first term, it is broadly true to say that the fulness of his direction was maintained. There was a good deal of confusion; there was muttering against his program; in one or two cases, there was even the threat of open revolt. But they came to nothing. "The victory of the president," wrote the most eminent of living American historians,[30] "was complete all along the line. . . . After the democratic processes of debate and confusion were given free rein, leadership emerged in the end. When results were surveyed at the end of the discussion and uproar, it could truly be said that seldom, if ever, in the long history of Congress had so many striking and vital measures been spread upon law books in a single session." The public seemed to confirm that view in the triumphant return of Mr. Roosevelt to power in the election of 1936.

But a change developed rapidly in the second term.

[29] Cf. E. P. Herring, *American Political Science Review*, Vol. 28, p. 70.
[30] Professor C. A. Beard in *Current History*, October, 1935, p. 64.

He was defeated over the Court plan. His first effort at administrative reorganization suffered a similar fate. In measures relating to relief and agriculture he was compelled to accept drastic changes. In the realm of foreign policy, at a vital juncture in international affairs, he was unable to secure acceptance of the proposals he made for changes in neutrality legislation which would have enlarged his discretionary powers. The Republicans gained heavily in the mid-term elections of 1938, and it was clear that the divisions in the ranks of the Democratic party jeopardized the president's control of it. Mr. Roosevelt could, indeed, at the adjournment of 1939, well have repeated Polk's complaint of ninety years before.[31] He had a nominal majority in both houses, but that majority was far more interested in maneuvers for the 1940 campaign than in the consideration of presidential policies. Complaints of presidential autocracy were loud even among members of the Democratic party; and the latter were prepared to enforce against the president the implications of senatorial courtesy over a judicial appointment even in a case where it was admitted that the proposed nominee was in every way appropriate for the position. It had become clear, in short, that with the disappearance of the more immediate gravities of the depression Congress generally, and the Senate in particular, was resentful of presidential leadership and eager to reduce it so far as they judged public opinion would permit. Mr. Roosevelt was not so disastrously placed as Mr. Wilson was in 1918; and

[31] *Op. cit.*, p. 186.

the brilliance of his maneuvers, combined with the depth of his personal hold on the electorate, combined to prevent Congress from going too far in its resentment. But there was nothing like the magical atmosphere of the first two years of his presidency. The desire of Congress to recover its authority was unmistakable. An attack upon presidential leadership was clearly becoming a primary issue of the political scene.

3

In the absence of special circumstances, this is to say, the hostility of Congress to the president is a part of its inner essence. Before we discuss its meaning, however, it is important to discuss the methods at the disposal of the president for influencing Congress. How does he get his way? What are the methods at his disposal for securing unity of outlook between the executive and the legislature?

One answer is to say at once that there is no general rule. Every president has his opportunities of influence; the way he uses them depends partly on his own personality and partly on the situation that he confronts. A president in an emergency is, obviously, likely to be far more influential than a president who, like Coolidge, is held to be ruling in a period of profound prosperity. A president whose party is in the majority in Congress has opportunities far greater than one who is in a minority in the House or the Senate or both. A president like McKinley, who knows Congress intimately, is obviously more likely to be successful in his handling of Congress than one who, like Mr. Hoover, is largely unaccustomed to its peculiar mental climate, and, in any case, unskilled in dealing with men. A president like John Quincy Adams, who is by nature aloof from public contact, is less likely to be successful than one who, like Theodore Roosevelt, has a genuine and instinctive liking for people. There is no general rule which enables one to predict with confidence that the relation between Congress and the president will be harmonious. Rather is it natural, on the record, to say that even if the normal conditions of harmony are present, at some stage strain is pretty certain to occur.

The first great element which makes for unity is the fact that the president and his party have a common interest in remaining in power. However great their differences, neither can do without the other. It is rarely enough for a man to be president; the drive that has placed him there makes him want to be a successful president; and this, in its turn, makes him seek to find the best terms of accommodation he can with his party. Usually, too, he wants renomination at the end of his first term; and this is always a strong ground for persuasion toward common ends. The party, too, needs the president. It lives by his record. To break with him in any thoroughgoing way is to risk the support of public opinion at the next election. Psychologically, the persistence of acute strain between the president and his party is always a major advantage to their opponents; it leads to defections from the ranks, and these, in doubtful areas, may be pivotal to the result. Senator Norris' loss to the Republican party in 1932, for example, undoubtedly brought many wavering voters to Mr. Roosevelt's side. And unity between them is important, too, in a material sense. A party lives by the spoils it has to distribute. The successful use of these is the condition of its effective organization. Unless some degree of harmony reigns between executive and legislature, there is always the danger that the advantages of office may be dissipated by their maldistribution.

It is important to realize that, the case of Andrew Johnson apart, no president has so far been completely deserted by his party. There have been grim periods of strain, as notably during the presidency of Tyler; but, in the end, some sort of outer harmony has been arranged. Deep, also, as the quarrel may be, it is rarely so deep, perhaps curiously, as between one party and another. I say curiously, because the line of cleavage between the parties is always more apparent than real; there is far more agreement between a progressive Republican like Senator La Follette and President Franklin Roosevelt than, say, between the former and Senator Hastings of Delaware. But it would take something like a constitutional revolution for Senator La Follette to emerge as a Democratic candidate for the presidency. Few Democrats were so critical of the Republican presidents of the last thirty years as the Republican Senator Borah; but he never "bolted" the party, and each presidential election found him offering at least a pinch of incense on the Republican altar.

A certain degree of harmony usually prevails in the first months of a presidential term. The incumbent is new to office; he has to feel his way; there is a general understanding, both in Congress and in public opinion, that he shall not be attacked until he is accustomed to his routine. This is not, indeed, always the case. Harding's death had hardly elevated Calvin Coolidge to the White House before the Senate rejected his nominee for the post of attorney-general, an event unprecedented in fifty years. In the first year of his administration they passed the soldiers' bonus over his veto. They refused to accept his view of Japanese immigration policy. They rejected his proposal of adherence to the World Court, and they mangled, despite a threatened veto, his super-tax proposals so that the body became a corpse. But this is comparatively rare. A president who has something real to say and do—the condition is important—can usually count on a "honeymoon period" in which what he asks for will, in large measure, have assurance of being granted. It is usually toward the close of his first congressional session that the buttons are taken off the foils.

The patronage, moreover, is an immense and necessary element in the making of this unity. Senators and congressmen want posts for their followers; and they know how much of their own future depends upon their ability to get them. To quarrel with the president may mean the withholding of the post from a man whose re-election begins to loom; it may even mean that a party rival in his own state or district becomes influential, with the possible result of his loss of the nomination at the next primary. It is the disposal of the patronage that keeps the party machinery oiled; and the loss of influence through opposition to the president may be a serious matter. President Cleveland used this weapon to force through the repeal of the Silver Purchase Act. President Wilson obtained the support of Senator Tillman for his most distinguished nomination to the Supreme Court by a similar method. Democrats who had waited for twelve long and hungry years for the patronage were easily stimulated, in the presence of crisis, to avoid discussion by an apt reminder from the president that the distribution would be delayed until the necessary measures were on the statute-book.[32] How vital an element in the retention of power the patronage may be is shown by the famous controversy between Garfield and Roscoe Conkling. Even a cabinet minister, as Polk has made plain,[33] may have "sleepless nights" because "the impression was becoming general . . . . that the patronage of the government here was being wielded against him." The immense extension of government service under President Franklin Roosevelt has not only been a direct cause of his great hold on Congress; its growth, also, has been a cause of Republican bitterness. It is natural to expect presidential influence to decline when the jobs have been distributed. But the Roosevelt policies have resulted in the creation of new agencies with large patronage almost

[32] Earle Looker, *The American Way* (1933), p. 67.
[33] *Op. cit.*, p. 40.

continuously through the administration of two terms. In these circumstances, exploitation of the differences between the president and his supporters in Congress has been a far more difficult matter than it usually is.

The president has also the veto power, in its various forms, as a method of influence. No one now accepts the view of Washington that a bill should be vetoed only upon the ground of its probable unconstitutionality. "If anything has been established by actual practice," wrote President Taft, "it is that the president, in signing a bill, or returning it unsigned, must consider the expediency and wisdom of the bill, as one engaged in legislation and responsible for it. The Constitution used the word 'approve,' and it would be a narrow interpretation to contract this into a mere decision as to legal validity."[34] This is the generally accepted view; even Benjamin Harrison, as much the mere agent of Congress as any president, vetoed seventeen measures. The president, he wrote,[35] "does not deal with bills submitted for his approval upon the principle that he should approve only such as he would have voted for if he had been a member of Congress. Much deference is due to the Congress, and vetoes have customarily been used only when the fault in the legislation was serious in itself or as a precedent." On the whole, it cannot be said that the power is a great one, or that it has been widely used; and Congress can always overrule the

[34] The Presidency (1916), pp. 13-14.
[35] This Country of Ours (1901), p. 133. On the general subject the best treatment is still E. C. Mason, The Veto Power (1890).

president by a two-thirds majority of the members who constitute a quorum in either house.[36] Eight presidents (seven of them in office before the Civil War) did not exercise their veto power at all. Of the earlier presidents, Washington exercised it twice, Madison on six occasions, and Monroe once. Jackson vetoed twelve measures and Tyler nine. In the post-Civil War period, Grant vetoed forty-three bills, Roosevelt forty, and Woodrow Wilson twenty-six. Cleveland vetoed no less than 358 measures; but the vast majority of them were private pension bills of an indefensible character. The passage of a bill over the president's veto is infrequent. No such passage occurred in the first fifty years of the republic. When it has been so passed, as with the Immigration Act of 1917 (which, in substantially the same form, had been vetoed successively by Cleveland, Taft, and Wilson), or the soldiers' bonus acts, passed over the vetoes of Coolidge, Hoover, and Franklin Roosevelt, the reason usually lies in the pressure of an organized opinion outside so strong that the Congress is not willing to take the risk of leaving the presidential veto as final.

The great defect in the veto power is the fact that it is total and not partial. The president must reject or accept a bill as a whole; he cannot, like the governors of several states, veto particular items and approve the rest. It is upon this fact that Congress has erected the gigantic structure of the "pork barrel" in general appropriation bills, and the device of

[36] *Missouri Pac. Ry. Co.* v. *Kansas* 248 U. S. 276 (1919).

[143]

the "rider" as an attachment thereto. Few presidents
will have the courage to veto this type of legislation,
objectionable though it be, simply because the failure
to secure necessary financial legislation hampers so
greatly the process of administration; though both
Taft and Wilson were brave enough to do so.[37]
President Grant vainly requested Congress to pass
an amendment giving him authority to veto parts of
bills. No doubt the new Budget Act of 1921 has effected some improvement in the financial powers of
Congress. But it is still true to say in this regard that
few financial measures go to the president for signa-
ture without items in them representing a gift to some
special interest for which no defense is possible and
which even the most lax president must be desirous
of expunging if he could. The veto power, in short,
though real, reaches but a little way. It will rarely be
exercised in that financial realm where it is most
needed; and, outside that realm, it mostly marks either
constitutional doubts on the part of the president's
advisers, or a difference between him and Congress
so acute that its exercise rather marks the degree of
strain than enables him to overcome it.

The real source, the patronage apart, of presidential power lies, ultimately, in the appeal to public
opinion. This power has a twofold source. On the
one hand, it derives from the fact of the president's
position; being the one element in the government

[37] In Wilson's case the rider, abolishing daylight saving, was passed
as a separate bill over his veto. The matter is now dealt with separately by each state.

which derives from the nation as a whole, it is natural
for it, especially in times of crisis, to look to him for
leadership. On the other, the public is naturally interested in the process of government; and a president of dominant personality can utilize that interest
to his advantage. Each of these sources deserves some
detailed exploration.

The position of the president in the national life
is hardly to be understood by anyone who has not
seen it both continuously and at first hand. For the
nation, while he is in office, he is in a real sense its
embodiment. It has made him president; that act of
creation gives him for it a reality and a respect quite
different in character from any that a hereditary mon-
arch possesses. Members of the nation may hate and
fear him; Franklin Roosevelt is, in some ways, the
most hated and feared president since Andrew Johnson. They may even despise him, as Calvin Coolidge
was frankly despised by a considerable number of
those who had any intimate contact with him. But,
fear or hate, or even contempt, there is inherent in
his office a sense of respect which brooks no denial.
It is a part of the make-up of the American citizen.
He can no more escape it than the Englishman can
escape the sense that royalty is somehow different
from ordinary clay. And because every American
has that sense, he looks up to the president, listens to
him, watches with attention his every action. The
president, by historic tradition, is placed on an eminence which not even so distinguished a figure as the
chief justice of the United States can rival. The

citizen may gossip about, and, as the various "whispering" campaigns have made clear, even against, the president. There may grow up, as in the case of President Coolidge, a whole saga of anecdotes about his habits. But the degree to which the president maintains interest, while he is president, even in the citizen most indifferent to politics, is an astonishing thing to the outsider.

The result is that he looks to the president for views. He expects leadership from him. He assumes that the president has opinions about every subject from the place of the Boy Scout movement in the national life to the problems of soil erosion. He expects consideration for those opinions. He expects his congressman or his senator to have opinions about those opinions. And because the president is not only the ceremonial head of the nation but also its executive head, he follows with some closeness what happens to presidential opinions upon matters of significant public import. Every president has an incomparable audience waiting for the pronouncement he may choose to make; to whomever else the Americans may not listen—and they are, in any case, a nation of listeners—they will listen to *him*. In any crisis, in the discussion of any big problem, they expect him to speak; in a very real sense, when he has spoken, they feel that the nation has spoken. To give a lead upon the issues of his time is not merely a constitutional function to be exercised in a formal way; it is, it increasingly becomes, an essential part of the presidential office. The more the president gives the lead, the greater the stature he assumes. He makes things intelligible, discussable almost, by speaking out. The people expect to be interested by their president; that is one of the reasons why they have elected him. They want to see him in action, to hear him speak. The foreigner may hear amusement, even contempt, about members of Congress; he will rarely hear anything but respect for the presidential office as such.

This attitude provides a basis which makes an appeal from the president to public opinion a matter of enormous significance. The audience is there to be interested; it is its president who speaks to it. No one else has the power that he has to mobilize public opinion; no one else can reach it so profoundly; no one else's judgment is, so decisively, "front page" news. The president, therefore, when he is at variance with Congress, starts with the advantage that there is a wide public opinion on his side. He is pretty sure to command a good deal of respect for his point of view; he is certain to command an interest with which no one else can compare. And a skilful president can, of course, maximize the opportunities at his disposal. His messages and speeches can prepare the ground. His press conferences are nothing so much as propaganda by which, through information and suggestion, he secures receptivity for his attitude. Phrases of his will become the current coin of conversation; Franklin Roosevelt's "horse and buggy" utterance has passed into the tradition of the nation. The effective use of the radio—which gives him almost the whole nation as an audience—offers him the certainty that his case will be heard and known as he wishes it heard and known. He has a means at his disposal for creating confidence in his point of view 'which far surpasses that at the disposal of any rival factor in the nation. He will be heard even if, as in the election of 1936, the overwhelming bulk of the press is opposed to him.

All this means that a president with the gift for leadership can, in Professor Cushman's phrase,[38] "usually find it possible to create a public sentiment . . . . which party leaders in and out of Congress dare not ignore." He must, of course, be determined and persistent. He must take care to see that the public mind is really concentrated upon his measure. He must have arguments on its behalf that are simple and direct and intelligible. He must avoid springing novelties upon the public which touch traditions which the record has—like that of the Supreme Court —made sacred. He must try to appear as the reasonable man battling against wilful obstinacy or vested interests. He must have, like Theodore Roosevelt, the power of accurate timing in his appeals, or, like Franklin Roosevelt, something akin to genius for making the complex appear simple and obvious. Even a dull president, like Rutherford Hayes, can arouse the nation if the fighting ground against him is badly chosen by Congress.[39] A president with a dominating temper can always be certain that if he has chosen

[38] *American National Government* (1931), p. 303.
[39] Cf. Burgess, *The Administration of President Hayes* (1916), pp. 65 f.

his issue well and phrased it skilfully he will win widespread popular support for his point of view. Granted, indeed, that the president really believes in his cause, and has persistency, he can so educate the nation in his support that a difficult case will make its way to victory.

There are many instances to prove this. The fight of Theodore Roosevelt for conservation is one example of it. The ability with which Woodrow Wilson took a united nation with him into the War of 1914 is another; for brilliance of timing, indeed, it would be difficult to surpass that achievement when it is remembered that, only five months before, the slogan "he kept us out of war" was one main cause of Wilson's re-election. Even Franklin Roosevelt's unsuccessful campaign against the Supreme Court prepared public opinion to believe that it was a reactionary body the composition of which was unsatisfactory; and this prepared the way for the virtually unanimous acceptance by the Senate of nominations which, but a short time before, would undoubtedly have been stoutly challenged. So, too, skilful use by the president of the congressional power of investigation may prepare the way, through the revelations it effects, for the acceptance of legislation which Congress itself is dubious about, and against which all the pressure of powerful "lobbies" is being exerted at the Capitol. The ruthless but salutary investigation of Wall Street at the hands of Judge Pecora undoubtedly made possible the drastic regulation of the New

York Stock Exchange.[40] It prepared the public mind for the notion that a cleansing was necessary by turning, under presidential inspiration, the pitiless light of publicity upon the habits of men who had previously seemed beyond the reach of public criticism. The pathetic appearance, under examination, of men like Andrew Mellon, "the greatest secretary of the treasury since Hamilton," broke the worship of idols whom it was necessary to break if the presidential policies were to be driven through Congress.

Obviously enough, great though the power is, there are limits to it. A president who offends certain deep traditions in the American mental climate will find that a recalcitrant Congress, if it is stubborn enough, can resist the pressures he can mobilize. A demand for innovation will, normally, force its way to acceptance in a crisis. But if habituation to the crisis develops, persistency in innovation may then break on the rock of older habituations the cultural lag of which has been stayed, rather than broken, by the crisis. This, I suspect, has been in part the explanation of the adverse fortune of Franklin Roosevelt with Congress since 1936. With the passage of the supreme emergency on the crest of whose wave he rode, certain normal American ideas, the divine right of the business man to be free from government interference, the idea of a balanced budget, the belief (now wholly untrue) that any energetic American can find a job if he really tries, that that government is best which spends least, that the budget ought to be

[40] Ferdinand Pecora, *Wall Street Under Oath* (1939).

balanced annually (an interesting fiscal superstition), have all resumed something of their wonted authority. The breakdown of business control gave the trade unions an immense opportunity, behind which the president put considerable pressure; and the National Labor Relations Act was the result. But American conditions have not, historically, been favorable soil for a strong trade union movement, and the reaction against its gains has, despite the president, made considerable headway in Congress. The president, in a word, can compel attention for the things he desires; but his chance of victory for those things is not one of which he can be certain. Almost always, his success depends upon the presence of a mental climate it is beyond his power to control.

His authority, moreover, is limited for another reason. Not only Congress grows anxious under a president who too frequently cracks the whip. Beyond it, there is always a powerful current of opinion adverse to a strong president as such. There is fear that the legislative branch of the government may be excessively dominated by the executive; that is un-American. It is pretty clear that some of the judges, of unquestionably liberal outlook, who shared in finding the National Industrial Recovery Act unconstitutional, were moved by fears that it conferred dangerously excessive powers of delegated legislation upon the president.[41] And there is a widespread fear, especially prevalent among farmers and business men of "too much government"; the tradition of laissez faire

[41] *Schechter v. U. S.*, 295 U. S. 495.

[151]

has still deep roots in the American consciousness. The period in which the realm of federal intervention was both narrow and expected to be narrow, is still near enough for such intervention to encounter the cross-current of suspicion that it is eroding that individual responsibility the anxiety for which is a legacy inherent in a civilization still hardly a generation distant from the traditions of the frontier.

The president, moreover, must pick his issues carefully. They must be wide enough to be genuinely interesting. They must be of the type that, emotionally, can be made pretty rapidly to seem important. They must, if possible, transcend the inherent sectionalism of Congress. And the appeal to the public must not be made too frequently. Just as an excessive use of the radio would dull its influence by making it over-familiar, so the president must not appear as a man who simply cannot "get on" with Congress. His case must be of the kind upon which the electorate is likely to feel strongly—strongly enough, at least, for them to feel that they must express themselves about it either in letters to the press or by personal communication with their senator or congressman. It must, too, be the kind of issue that is familiar enough in its general outline to have a historic basis upon which presidential sentiment can be built up. When Franklin Roosevelt pressed for the Securities and Exchange Act, he had behind him the memories, far from dim, of Theodore Roosevelt's thunder against "malefactors of great wealth," and Woodrow Wilson's "new freedom" for the little man. When he protested against the Nazi rape of Czecho-Slovakia, he could rely, not only upon the still vivid memories of the war years, but upon the deep emotions of a large number of Czech-Americans to whom the rebirth of their native land in 1918 had been one of the two or three supreme public events in their lives.

The success of the president, I have said, often depends upon factors outside his control. The immense complications of the neutrality tangle of 1938-39 are interesting evidence of this. The president is searching for a free hand. He confronts in Congress an opposition, largely reflected in the country at large, which is compounded of a variety of factors. Some of it is the traditional demand for American isolation; Washington's warning against "permanent alliances" is still one of which every president must take account. Some of it is due to the revelations of congressional inquiries, of which that of Senator Nye into the armaments industry is perhaps outstanding, that have made many Americans—not least those of liberal temper—fearful of what the free hand may, in practice, conceal. Some of it, no doubt, is due to a suspicion that there is not so much to choose between Herr Hitler and Mr. Chamberlain; the profound psychological impact of Munich upon American opinion is unquestionable, especially upon that liberal opinion so important to Mr. Roosevelt. A good deal of it is sheer maneuvering for position in the next presidential election; the more the president can be discredited by defeat the less will he be a vital factor when that issue is determined.

Yet none of these factors is a tithe so important as what may happen in Europe itself. The issue of American neutrality will be largely determined by the limits of the aggression attempted by the Fascist powers.

4

To what conclusions does this argument lead? First, I think, it should be noted that a distinction must be drawn between the "crisis" situation and the "normal" situation. In the first, the president's position is so overwhelming that it is, broadly, imperative for Congress to follow where he chooses to lead. Then, the nation requires action, and it looks to the president to define the kind of action that is required. It assumes the necessity, in crisis, for the conference upon him of wide powers; it is impatient of doubt about, or hostility to, their conference. It may, indeed, almost be said that it is too impatient; no one can analyze, for instance, the workings of the Espionage Act of 1917 without seeing that Congress then practically abdicated before the president.[42] Much the same is true of the "hundred days" of Franklin Roosevelt. It would have been literally impossible, in the face of public opinion, for Congress to have resisted the pressure to give the president what he chose to demand; there are, indeed, careful observers who believe that if, at that moment, he had demanded even so drastic a measure as the nationalization of the banks, Congress would have had to accept it. In a

[42] Cf. Walter Nelles, *Espionage Act Cases* (1920), and Z. C. Chaffee, *Freedom of Speech* (1920).

crisis, to put it shortly, public opinion compels the abrogation of the separation of powers. There is really only one will in effective operation, and that is the will of the president. He is as powerful, while the emergency has a psychological hold on the country, as the British prime minister at a moment of national emergency.

But in a "normal" situation the position is very different. The American system, in its ultimate foundations, is built upon a belief in weak government. It must never be forgotten that the Constitution is the child of the eighteenth century; that the influence of Locke and Montesquieu is written deeply into its clauses. Those who made it were, out of actual and inferred experience, above all afraid of arbitrary power. They constructed a system of checks and balances as a bulwark against its emergence. They did so because they believed, with Madison, that "the accumulation of powers in a single hand is the very definition of tyranny." They did so because the effective citizen whom they were above all considering was the bourgeois man of adequate property who needed protection, on the one hand against an ambitious executive, and on the other against a legislature unduly under the influence of the propertyless mob. Naturally enough, in their day, the good state seemed to be the negative state. They were not unduly enamored of democracy, even if few of them would have said openly with Alexander Hamilton that the people was "a great beast." They believed profoundly in fundamental law; and their interpretation of its substance, whether they were Federalists like John Marshall or Democrats like Thomas Jefferson, was that it guaranteed their conception of the rights of property against legislative invasion. The state they constructed was the negative state that a nation of small property owners required; the state, be it noted, that under similar pressures, if in different form, was being simultaneously created in England and in France. The nineteenth century seemed, in large degree, to vindicate their notions; for, slavery apart, the immense physical resources at the disposal of the nation saved it from the deep social tensions of Europe for nearly a hundred years after 1787. It was not until such a period as the Haymarket Riots that an observer could claim general acceptance for the view that there was no qualitative difference between the problems of America and those of Europe. The remarkable insights of men like Orestes Brownson[43] fell upon ears largely deaf. He was speaking of class conflict when little else could be perceived but that contest over slavery which, by its intensity, seemed to transcend all other forms of social difference.

The idea of weak government fitted into the pattern of the first century of American development. It was aided by the facts, first, that the major parties were dominated by business men whom that idea suited; and second, that until the turn of the century trade unions were not a serious force to be reckoned with

[43] There is now a good biography of this remarkable man by Arthur Schlesinger Jr., *Orestes Brownson* (1939); see also an excellent analysis by Helen Mims in *Science and Society*, Spring, 1939.

in American politics. Legislative experiments in a positive direction were hampered at every turn by the courts filled predominantly by judges whose ideas of constitutional validity were shaped by devotion to the ideal of the negative state. Until almost the time of Woodrow Wilson, it is not unfair to describe the Senate as a rich man's club; and the attitude of Theodore Roosevelt to what now appear to be the very moderate ideas of the elder La Follette makes it obvious that the difficulties against which positive ideas in social legislation had to struggle were very great.[44] The power, moreover, of the business forces over the parties was immense; the history both of the Bryan campaign and of the Progressive movement is evidence of that. Even if the farmers were, on occasion, tempted "to raise less corn and more hell," they were uninterested in problems—the hours of labor, for example—which went beyond their narrow horizon. The disposition of forces in American politics, in short, all made toward the idea of a government which did not disturb those conditions of confidence which business men approved.

It was to the maintenance of those conditions that Congress largely directed its attention. On examination, it will be found that practically every major occasion in which there has been conflict between Congress and the president was, from Jackson onward, an occasion when the policy of the president seemed likely to disturb them. With Jackson, it was the bank; with Andrew Johnson, it was the fulfilment of the

[44] Cf. Pringle, *op. cit.*, pp. 547-548.

triumph of the industrial North against the agrarian South; with Theodore Roosevelt and Woodrow Wilson, it was a struggle against monopolies, with Franklin Roosevelt, it has been an effort to subdue the operations of business enterprise to a larger social purpose. In each case, also, the structure of the American Constitution, by dividing initiative in policy, through the legacy of a belief that weak government is desirable, has confused that initiative. The result has mainly been a compromise satisfactory to neither side. Few presidents, except in emergency, have secured what they sought; few Congresses have been able to prevent all they have desired to prevent from being enacted. No plan of action has been legislated coherently, or administered coherently. No allocation of direct responsibility for failure on either head has been seriously possible.

For once the need for a positive state began to be admitted—as it was reluctantly admitted in the presidency of Theodore Roosevelt—one outstanding principle was clear. It was the principle, long ago adumbrated by John Stuart Mill, that the formulation of legislative proposals is not a task for which a legislature is fitted. A legislature can criticize; it can ventilate grievance; its power to investigate through committees is invaluable; and, not least, as it fulfils these tasks it provides a process of public education which is pivotal to democratic government. But a legislature like Congress is at once too big and too incoherent of itself to devise an organic and unified approach to the problems of the time. It is not effectively organized to take a continuous initiative. Its members are not compelled to think by their position in terms of the problems of the whole nation. Each house of Congress has a separate prestige; their common prestige is, by their nature, inherently anti-presidential in character. To be something, Congress is forced to take a stand against the president; it cannot be anything if it merely follows his lead. And the weakness of the system is magnified by the fact that though it can seek its own elevation only by discrediting him, it cannot destroy him. He is there, whether it will or no, for his term; and his power to appeal against its decisions is but interstitial in character. The result of the system, normally, is therefore to dissipate strength rather than to integrate it. The president is usually less than he might be, because the stature of Congress is diminished the more fully he has his way; and Congress is never all that it might become, because it is so organized as to prevent the acceptance of clear sailing directions.

It is, of course, true that the ties of party provide a barrier against the consequences of this dissipation of strength. The president and his supporters have always a common interest in getting something done because their record measures the chance of later success at the polls. Yet that common interest is tempered by a number of hindrances. It is hindered by the fact that the committee system makes a number of little presidents, as it were, in the congressional sphere; there is a dual quasi-executive within the legislature, even though it does not enjoy executive power.

It is hindered again by the fact that, as the president's term draws to its close, the temptation to withdraw from him what allegiance the party system enforces is maximized. If the president, like Hayes, is not seeking re-election at the end of his first term, his power is likely to be small. "The very fact," writes Professor Commager,[45] "that Hayes was not a candidate for re-election accentuated the question of the succession, and bedevilled his administration with some of the most bitter political conflicts in our history—intra-party conflicts into which Hayes himself was drawn." And it is notable that the second term of those presidents who have been re-elected has in each case been less creative than the first. The problem of the succession means far more to congressional politics than the fruits of the legislative process.

No president is in a position to prevent this disintegration in normal times; even Washington could not do so, for it was in his second term that the forces were aligned which ultimately became the Federalist and Republican parties. An American party is not a unity in the English sense; it is a loose confederation of interests each of which is playing for power. It is therefore engaged, not merely in a fight against the opposing party, but also in a fight against factions within itself. No president can be sure that he will not have to pay the price for that factionalism. "I learned tonight," wrote Polk, on the twenty-first of

[45] See his illuminating article, "One, Two, or Three Terms," New York Times Magazine, July 23, 1939.

April, 1846,[46] "that the Senate, by the votes of Mr. Calhoun and his wing of the Democratic party, united with the whole Whig party, had rejected the nomination of Dr. Amos Nourse as collector. . . . This is, in addition to other evidence, a pretty clear indication that Mr. Calhoun intends to oppose my administration. He has embarrassed the administration on the Oregon question. He is playing a game to make himself president. . . ." On June 24, 1846, he is complaining of further rejections through the influence of certain senators. "The sooner," he comments,[47] "such party men go into the ranks of the Whig party, the better." "Democratic and Whig senators," he writes on February 28, 1848,[48] ". . . . act solely with the view to the elevation of themselves or their favorites to the presidential office. . . . Senators act as if there was no country and no public interests to take care of." Many later presidents must have re-echoed these sentiments.

In "normal" times, indeed, the relation between the president and Congress has a curious analogy with that between the French governments of the Third Republic and the Chamber of Deputies. No doubt, there is far greater executive stability in the American system; the Constitution provides for that. But there is in both an incoherence and irresponsibility in the relations between executive and legislature which it is impossible not to remark; in both, also, factionalism tends

[46] *Op. cit.*, p. 72.
[47] *Op. cit.*, p. 117.
[48] *Op. cit.*, p. 313.

greatly to destroy the prospect that any government may hope continuously to drive through an ample program of social change. In both, also, embarkation upon that program results in a withdrawal of business confidence; and a reforming government is presented with the alternatives of recovery or reform. In both, too, the individual legislator is prone to take every opportunity to mark his independence of the executive; and his support, only too often, has to be purchased by administrative favors. Both show, especially in the last generation, the striking phenomenon of "normal" governments being succeeded, every so often, by "crisis" governments, in which legislative irresponsibility compels the conference of wide powers upon the executive as a remedy for the irresponsibility. In both, also, a return to "normality" produces a return to the earlier characteristics. Neither shows any propensity to embark upon those fundamental reforms which the incoherence and instability suggest as imperative.

It may, of course, be said that the present system in the United States has served it well enough for a century and a half; that each crisis has demonstrated on the part of Congress a willingness to confer sufficient powers upon the president to cope with it. The answer to this view is, I think, twofold. It is, in the first place, clear that the basis of an institutional system framed for a negative state cannot easily be adequately adapted to the needs of a positive state. The legislative program in the latter type of organization needs an integration and a coherent continuity that it cannot attain under the American system; more, it requires standards of administrative performance and experience which cannot be improvised every four or eight years. And in the second place, no democracy in the modern world can afford a scheme of government the basis of which is the inherent right of the legislature to paralyze the executive power. Presidential programs often suffer from grave inadequacies; presidential leadership is often smaller than the problems it confronts. However inadequate, and however small, they are the only programs and leadership which are projected upon a national plane; more, they alone are so operated in the open as to focus upon themselves the whole force of public opinion. The weakness of the relationship established between the president and Congress is that it gives the latter a constant interest in the diminution of his power. It is not merely that, so to say, he is on the way out as he is on the way in. It is also that the sanctions he possesses are not continuous enough in their operation to make his leadership continuously effective except under conditions the avoidance of which is the purpose of every scheme of government. Whatever the weaknesses of the British system, it makes responsibility for action clear and direct and intelligible. An executive which cannot command the confidence of the legislature may appeal beyond it to the electorate. So long as it controls the legislature, its authority is coherent and integrated. These are immense advantages. The authority may be abused; but at least the responsibility for the abuse is always clearly indicated. The energy of the executive is not continually dissipated in patching up the majorities it requires for some degree of the program it has urged. The allegiance of its supporters is not constantly shifting on its axis. There is not a continuous interest in the legislature to develop a policy of its own at the cost of executive credit.

No doubt a good deal in the American pattern is easily explicable in historical terms. But that still leaves open the vital question whether past history is an excuse for present inadequacy. The modern state requires disciplined leadership; the American system leaves no assurance of its continuous availability. It is, indeed, built upon foundations that are inherently suspicious of leadership as such. From the foundation of the republic, as we can see from the pages of Maclay's *Diary*, the president has run in the leading strings of congressional control. This control has not presented a clear alternative to his leadership. Rather, for the most part, its result has been a confusion of the public mind. He may move in one direction; that is almost an invitation to Congress to move in several other directions. The clash of opinion about the wisdom of the alternative he emphasizes does not lead back to the people from whom his authority emanates. Rather does it result in an interregnum of power while the forces in opposition are maneuvering for an advantage they can only seize at stated intervals without chronological coincidence with national necessity.

These are momentous difficulties which reach down into the foundations of the Constitution. They are not touched, I venture to think, by any of the minor expedients of reform that have so far been proposed. The central problem of representative government in a democracy is, I repeat, to make the source of responsibility for action unmistakable, and to reach at once that citizen-body whose verdict upon its exercise is alone decisive. That problem, I suggest, is not solved in the American system. Its very nature is to dissipate responsibility by substituting the politics of maneuver for the politics of policy. No doubt, as Adam Smith said, there is a great deal of ruin in a nation; and emergency will always force a unity upon forces which the system is constructed to divide. But a government does not prove its adequacy because it can transcend its own principles in an emergency; its adequacy is born of its ability to prevent the outbreak of emergency. That is the test by which the relationship between the president and Congress must be judged. At the least, there are grounds for grave doubt whether it can meet this test successfully.

IV

FOREIGN RELATIONS

I

IF NO democratic people has yet satisfactorily
solved the problem of its control of foreign relations, it can at least be said that nowhere has a more
careful effort been made toward that end than in
the United States. The president may have immense
powers in negotiation; but in the ultimate disposition
of its result he is the subject of the Senate before whose
power of veto and amendment he must bow. Where
the House of Commons is, in this realm, the virtual
creature of any government that is not the author of
overt disaster, the Senate of the United States is in a
position at least to scrutinize every step of the executive, and, in large degree, to control its outcome. It
cannot be said, I think, that a satisfactory balance between the president and the Senate has so far been
attained; indeed it is in a real sense difficult to state their
relations in any precise way. For, in the first place,
ever since the administration of Washington a controversy has been proceeding between them as to the
exact degree of power each is entitled to exercise;
and, in the second, the relation changes as the international situation contributes a different emphasis to

American history. Different presidents, moreover, have viewed their foreign problems quite differently, and this, also, has changed the emphasis. But whatever the international situation, and whoever has occupied the presidential office, it can, I think, be truly said that no legislative assembly in the world rivals the Senate of the United States in its influence in the international sphere.

The provisions of the Constitution give but a partial index to the nature of the relationship. The president, it lays down, "shall have power, by and with the consent of the Senate, to make trea..es, provided two-thirds of the senators present concur."[1] Negotiation is the prerogative of the president; but the treaty is binding upon the citizens of the United States only with the consent of the Senate. There is a sense, also, in which the relation of the House of Representatives to a treaty is important; for no money can be raised to complete its implementation without the consent of that house. The declaration of war, moreover, is a joint act of both houses. The Senate, further, is directly concerned in foreign relations since it must confirm the appointment of all ambassadors and other diplomatic representatives. This is the formal framework of the structure as the founders of the Constitution defined it. I need not say that it supplies but a partial clue to the grasp of the whole network of relations that have been built upon it.

It may fairly be said that two substantial principles emerge upon which the whole presidential relation to

[1] Art. II, Sec. 2, clause 2.

foreign affairs has been built. The first cannot be better stated than in the classic words of Thomas Jefferson: "The transaction of business with foreign nations is executive altogether." This, as a general rule, has come to be the accepted practice of the United States. Apart from that process of approval and consent of which the Constitution speaks, whether in relation to instruments or persons, it is the president who decides what degree of consultation shall precede the formal submission of the result of his negotiations. From this wide freedom there follows, I think logically, the second principle that Congress, and above all the Senate, shall not be prejudiced constitutionally in the exercise of its powers in its own sphere, by what the president has done in his. No doubt, in fact, there is continuous reciprocity of influence. But that is not held to deter either authority from independent action in its allotted field.

This allocation of functions has, in fact, come to mean that the president has a decisive hand in the shaping of foreign affairs, even though the Congress, and especially, of course, the Senate, retains a negative voice. He is considerably dependent upon the secretary of state, whose department has grown from the four clerks, a French interpreter, and two messengers under Jefferson to some six hundred officials in Washington and some three thousand employed all over the world. But exactly as the prime minister of Great Britain has a specially close relation to, even supremacy over, the foreign secretary, so it has been the case, in general, for the president of the United States to

take the main hand in shaping at least the large outlines of foreign policy. Some presidents, indeed, like
Jefferson, Polk, Theodore Roosevelt, and Woodrow
Wilson, have been, to all intents and purposes, their
own secretaries of state; others, like Harding and
Coolidge, have left a large discretion to the State Department. Woodrow Wilson seems to have allowed
Mr. Bryan some elbowroom in the field of the latter's
special hobby of arbitration, while retaining a general
oversight of his work; and I suspect that this would
not be an unfair description of the relations between
Mr. Hull and President Franklin Roosevelt. Great
men, no doubt, whose collaboration it has not been
easy to subjugate, have presided over the State Department; five of them subsequently became presidents,
two chief justices, while three others, Clay, Webster and Calhoun, are among the outstanding figures
in American history. Nevertheless, one cannot read
the essential documents without the clear inference
that the overmastering impulses in foreign affairs derive from the presidential mind. An occasional president may be content to play a secondary role; but I
do not think this can be said of more than four presidents, and, with all but Grant, foreign affairs played
a comparatively minor part in his administration.
Whatever the degree of consultation with his colleagues, in the cabinet or in Congress, the president remains the chief architect in this field.

This can be seen if we consider briefly the range of
his initiative. It is for him to choose, and to dismiss,
his chief collaborators; the secretary of state who does

not agree with him must go. The ambassador with whom he is not satisfied may, like Mr. Page, remain in office; but it is a sufficient commentary upon his influence that, after Mr. Wilson's death, a great mass of Page's letters to him were discovered unopened. The president has unlimited discretion in the recognition of new governments. How powerful that influence has been in the recent history of Mexico it is unnecessary to emphasize. But it has had, also, an immense influence in the history of Europe; Franklin Roosevelt's recognition of the Soviet government, for example, may well prove to have been a real turning point in its history, as may his refusal so far[2] to recognize the Japanese conquest of Manchuria or the German absorption of Czecho-Slovakia. He has a wide and undefined authority to send special agents abroad; the part played by Colonel House in the European War of 1914-18 is only the supreme example of policies shaped and understandings secured by this means. He has an undefined power, further, to enter into compacts that are less than treaties without the participation of the Senate; the consequence of this power may be only slightly less than actual entrance into a treaty. He has the exclusive and unchallengeable right to negotiate treaties up to the point of their acceptance by the Senate; though here it should be added that history, especially the history of the Treaty of Versailles, makes the lesson clear that in treaty-making full consultation with at least the vital figures in the Senate Committee on Foreign Affairs is pivotal to the suc-

[2] August, 1939.

cessful conclusion of any treaty which arouses serious debate. He has a wide initiative in the official formulation of the national foreign policy; and though, no doubt, this is in some degree a hazardous political adventure, there is no field in which the president has so full an opportunity of giving a lead. No European, certainly, of my own generation is likely to forget how Woodrow Wilson, between 1917 and 1919, voiced in his public utterances the aspirations of the common people all over the world. The president, moreover, is the commander-in-chief of the armed forces of the United States. In that aspect, he may legitimately take action, as the history of Mexico bears ample witness, which leaves Congress no alternative but to follow the lead he has chosen to give.

I am summarizing too briefly a vast range of function. It must be understood that in each of its aspects, especially in a critical time, the whole world is watching with attention the direction a president may follow. There is no doubt, for example, that British policy in the Far East at the present moment is largely conditioned by the president's attitude to Japanese aggression in China. There is little doubt, either, that the Fascist powers had, for a long time, been largely deterred from risking a European war by fear that Mr. Roosevelt might persuade America to place at least its boundless material resources at the service of the democracies. The leadership provided by the president in foreign affairs is, without any doubt, the pivotal influence in framing foreign policy. Whatever part the Constitution may assign to the legislative agency, the spirit of the presidential purpose, especially in a situation of gravity, is the overwhelming factor in forming the direction and the decision.

It is, of course, inevitable that it should be so. Whatever may have been the intention of the founders, the framing of foreign policy and its negotiation cannot be carried on by a numerous assembly. The interviews, the documentation, the understandings of personal intercourse all forbid it. Some degree of secrecy is inescapable in matters of international intercourse; anyone, for instance, can see that negotiations like those for an Anglo-Soviet pact could not be carried on to the accompaniment of full public discussion at each of its stages; a proposal of marriage must be made in private, even if the engagement is later discussed in public. That the balance of diplomatic power should, therefore, be in the president's hands, arises almost from the nature of things.

It is, of course, a limited power. The Senate has very fully maintained its right to confirm treaties, to reject them, or to amend them before offering its concurrence. The House of Representatives has always insisted upon its right to refuse appropriations which become necessary under ratified and confirmed treaties; though I believe it has never exercised that right. The Congress has insisted, as with the Russian Treaty of 1911, upon its power to abrogate treaties. Acts of Congress may also limit the presidential initiative; in 1939, for example, the area within which the president might maneuver was clearly limited by the implications of the Neutrality Act of 1937. In an extreme instance the fact that a declaration of war must be made by both houses of Congress is a safeguard against a supreme presidential indiscretion. Seward, for instance, was in favor of declaring war against France and Spain to cement the union; had he persuaded Lincoln to accept his view, the result might have been grave indeed. Against misjudgment of that kind, the congressional power is a check, even if its limits are obvious.

Taken as a whole, the record of American presidents in the making of foreign policy is a remarkable one. There have been, no doubt, the heavy sins of "dollar diplomacy"; this is not, however, a realm in which a European can afford to cast the first stone. There has been a good deal of brag and bluster, as with Polk over the Oregon boundary, with Cleveland over Venezuela, with the quite indefensible actions of Theodore Roosevelt in the diplomatic prelude to the building of the Panama Canal. If, indeed, there is a general case to be made against presidential leadership in foreign affairs, it is less upon the grounds of policy than upon the grounds of the defective organization he has built for informing himself about the affairs of foreign nations. In the post-Civil War period, American diplomatic representation in at least the major states has been the reward for standing in the party, often financial standing only, rather than for *expertise* in foreign affairs. A rich newspaper proprietor, the owner of a large department store, the husband of a great heiress to a fortune made in patent foods, have, to take stray examples, been accounted adequate holders of posts which, in most other countries, go only to men who have proved their fitness by long political or diplomatic experience. An embassy, perhaps, is less important in the days of the transatlantic telephone than it was when Jefferson and Monroe and Charles Francis Adams made the place of the United States so formidable in diplomatic discussion by their skill and force. This may explain the increasing tendency of the president to rely for the information he requires upon the special envoy, often appointed outside the categories which require senatorial confirmation, on the ground that he enjoys in a peculiar degree the private confidence of the president. But, for reasons I have already suggested, I think the development an unfortunate one. Its tendency is necessarily toward the choice of men whose contacts are not only interstitial, but who are almost bound, like Colonel House, to be "yes-men" for the president in order to retain their influence with him. They tend, therefore, as the *House Papers* make evident, to see mainly what the president wants them to see; and they lack that independence and responsibility which are the hallmarks of the expert diplomatist.

The record of the presidents, I have said, is on the whole remarkably good in foreign policy, and it is worth while speculating why this should have been the case. With the earlier presidents, it is easy to understand. From Washington to Monroe, every president, by the experience through which he had passed, had received a severe schooling in the technique of diplomatic intercourse. That was true, also, of John Quincy

Adams, whose claim to the authorship of the Monroe Doctrine is no small one. From Jackson to the Civil War, the main pressure of foreign policy is concerned with affairs within the American hemisphere—Mexico, the Oregon boundary, and so on; in each of these, either the power of the United States as against any possible opponent was overwhelming, or, as with the Oregon boundary question, it was dealing with an antagonist who was always eager for an honorable compromise. The Civil War, indeed, presented questions to the president of great delicacy and magnitude; and there is no more remarkable proof of the inherent and inescapable greatness of Lincoln than in the study of his alterations of Seward's dispatches.[3] After Lincoln, there was no president until Cleveland with any close grip on foreign affairs; Grant's handling of the Santo Domingo problem is merely one of many proofs of his unfitness for the presidential office. But from Cleveland onward, it is, I think, true to say that only Harding and Coolidge showed an ignorance of and unfitness for the control of foreign affairs; though in each case those defects were merely particular instances of a general incapacity. Theodore Roosevelt may have had, to excess, the Palmerstonian truculence, and in a less degree this is true of Cleveland also. But both Woodrow Wilson and Franklin Roosevelt showed, in this realm, a capacity to speak in world-terms which has already given them a special place in history; while

[3] Mr. Justice Holmes, who as a young officer in the Civil War knew Lincoln personally, was fond of telling how he first realized the greatness of Lincoln by the study of these dispatches.

the limited opportunities Mr. Hoover had showed him, in this aspect, as a man capable of wide perspectives. American foreign policy is, by reason of the processes in which it is involved, a thing far more complex to make effectively than is the case in Europe. The grasp, therefore, which presidents have held upon it is all the more striking.

The reasons, I suggest, are complicated. In the first place, it is so because the president is not, as Lord Bryce thought, likely to be merely an "available" man. The capacities which make him president are likely, therefore, to be displayed in foreign affairs as in other realms. The remoteness, further, of America from Europe and the Far East gives him in relation to their problems a sense of poise which is less easily attainable by the statesmen of other powers. And it is important that in the United States, differently from in Europe, foreign affairs are party problems in a high degree. The president, therefore, who seeks success in this realm has to rely far more on public opinion than is the case elsewhere; and to rely upon it, he has to educate it. Anyone who watched the process by which Woodrow Wilson brought a united nation into the war of 1914-18, or who has scrutinized narrowly the effort of Franklin Roosevelt to persuade the American people into the acceptance of his views, will realize how large a part the factor of public opinion plays. It does so for another reason. America is an amalgam of the most diverse national strains. Each of them has not only its special views on foreign policy; more important, each of them is likely to have a spokesman in

Congress whose views will count. And what is true of national strains is true also, if in a lesser degree, of religious faiths. American policy to tsarist Russia was profoundly influenced by anti-Jewish pogroms there; Franklin Roosevelt, in his attitude to the Spanish Civil War of 1936-39 was deeply influenced, perhaps over-influenced, by the knowledge of an immense Roman Catholic population in the United States; Protestant missionary zeal has had a considerable effect on policy in Turkey and China. The delicacy involved in handling these interests has, almost of itself, been a training in diplomatic technique; and to this must be added the fact that a wise president learns from his dealings with Congress many of the qualities which are important in international intercourse.

Yet in the postwar years, I think the source of presidential authority has lain in two different directions. There can be little doubt, despite his defeat over the Peace of Versailles, that the emergence during the war of Woodrow Wilson as a world-figure equaled only by Lenin has given the American people an interest in foreign politics which provides the president with an audience for his ideas upon them greater than at any previous time. No one who saw the almost painful intensity with which every move of the Czech crisis in September, 1938, was followed throughout the United States can doubt that this is the case. And because there is this interest, the notion of the president as the leader of the nation has come to have a special relevance in foreign affairs. He is expected to play a big part there. The citizen looks to his pronouncements with exceptional anxiety. He has the sense, as never before, that America is a world-power, and that his president must play his part in a manner proportionate to the influence of the United States in world affairs. This attitude is new in its intensity; but its beginnings can be traced back to the presidency of Theodore Roosevelt. In the aftermath of the Spanish-American War, men began to realize that the part America was to play was different from anything that they had previously expected. They felt that a new epoch had arrived in their destiny. They had colonies; they were exporting capital; they had begun to have, as in China, spheres of special influence. There grew up in America even before the war the consciousness of a world-destiny; and this consciousness has been profoundly reflected in the attitude of the presidents.

I do not think this conclusion is vitiated by the fact that every president, in his endeavor, if he will, to play this world-part, is confronted by a profound isolationism which affects considerable areas of the country. We are told that the Middle West and the Far West are uninterested in European affairs; and we are bidden to remember that no president, as he frames a world-policy, can neglect the immense influence of, for example, German, Italian, and Irish settlers. I do not think he can neglect them; there is a real truth and significance in Henry Adams' picture of Senator Lodge scouring round Washington to do favors for Irish and Greek constituents.[4] But I think that their influence can easily be exaggerated. In the first place,

4 *The Education of Henry Adams* (1918), p. 419.

the experience of Woodrow Wilson suggests very clearly that great leadership in a president can always transcend the power of these elements in a great emergency. In the second place, the interest of the West in Far Eastern issues is profound; and these become daily more related, and are understood to be related, to European problems. The United States, moreover, is now, for good or ill, an exporting country in which the influence of international finance is fundamental; and this plays a part in pushing any president toward a leadership likely, I think, to grow more, and not less, significant. Nor must one forget that every national group which pushes him to isolationism is usually counterbalanced by another national group which is pushing him against it. In the result, I think he is bound to choose a position which gives his people as a whole the sense, not only that the United States has something important to say on world-problems, but that it has power enough behind what it says to compel the world to listen.

The president, in fact, shapes and voices the foreign policy of the United States to a degree that no other competing power can rival. The treaty-making power apart—I shall discuss this later—he is, subject to the influence of public opinion, incomparably the master of the field. His speeches have an influence that is supreme. His ambassadors act under his instructions. It is with him that foreign ministers must engage in the give-and-take of diplomatic intercourse. And we must never forget that he is the commander-in-chief of the armed forces of the United States. What this means the experience of the Central and South American republics has made constantly manifest. What it means, also, was shown by the decision of Franklin Roosevelt, in the spring of 1939, to concentrate the major American fleet in the Pacific; that has had a palpable influence at least upon the Japanese attitude to American interests in the Far East and possibly beyond that sphere. His ability to make "understandings" short of treaties counts for a good deal, as witness Theodore Roosevelt's relations with Japan and Panama and Santo Domingo. There is an immense authority latent in his power of recognition. I do not for a moment say that he has unlimited power; pretty clearly, he must keep in step with the predominant public opinion he encounters. But I do not think that anyone can survey the record of those presidents who have deliberately sought influence in foreign affairs, and deny that he has immense power to shape the public opinion he will encounter. That was true of Polk; it was true of Cleveland; it was true of Theodore Roosevelt and of Woodrow Wilson. I think it has been true, also, of Franklin Roosevelt.

For I do not think it would be easy to deny that, in the momentous years since 1933, the president's attitude to the dictator-powers has carried immense weight with his people. He has trained them to an expectancy that he will act; and they have been led to look to him for action. It has, no doubt, been true that he has not been able, as the debate over neutrality legislation has made clear, to persuade them as far as he himself would probably have wished. But what I

think the historian will observe in the record is the
fact that each of his initiatives in these years has
widened the gulf between the support he can elicit
and that gained by those in opposition to him. He may
lose, as it were, particular battles; he retains, and is
understood to retain, the power of the offensive in the
campaign. Partly, that is the outcome of his persistence. He is at the task every day; the attention of
his opponents is continually diverted by other interests. Partly, also, and very importantly, the play of the
drama is on his side. He can see, as his opponents cannot see, several moves ahead in the maneuver for position. He has the papers; he engages in the conversa-
tions; he can strike at the moment when emotions
grow hot. It is immensely important, as a psychological factor in the exercise of his potential power,
that at each pivotal moment in the drama people ask:
"What is the United States going to do?" And that is,
in effect, to ask what the president is going to do. So
long as this remains the case, he is bound, almost, to
give some sort of lead. The authority at his disposal
is immense and elastic. He is in the position in which
his own people would, in these circumstances, feel
that a refusal to play a part was not merely his personal abdication but that of the United States also.
So that, in effect, its prestige is embodied in him. He
can loose, and he can be sure that he can loose, the
immense forces behind that prestige. He may, indeed,
later on pay the price for loosing them, as Woodrow
Wilson did over the rejection of the Peace of Versailles. And I do not for a moment deny that he courts

defeat by the risks he has to take. My point is the different one that he is compelled by his position to take the risks, and that, if in his judgment it is wise to take them, it is improbable that anyone can say him nay. "The transaction of business with foreign powers," to repeat Jefferson's phrase, "is executive altogether." Because that is the case, all the fundamental relations in the building of foreign policy are in his hands. It is a field in which, in a vital sense, his discretions are acts upon which it is difficult to go back. In no other part of American political life has the separation of powers counted for so little as in the definition of this part.

2

This is a conclusion too rarely emphasized in the books. Attention, especially since the famous struggle over the Peace of Versailles, has been concentrated on the treaty-making power of the Senate; and the heaviest artillery that academic research could concentrate has been trained on the exercise of that power.[5] Critics have pointed out the scale upon which the

[5] The best general discussion is in Professor Lindsay Rogers' brilliant treatise, *The American Senate* (1926), pp. 84-87. For fuller and very important discussion see also G. H. Haynes, *The Senate of the United States* (1938), II, 569-720; R. J. Dangerfield, *In Defense of the Senate* (1933); W. Stull Holt, *Treaties Defeated by the Senate* (1933); D. F. Fleming, *The Treaty Veto of the American Senate* (1930). The early history in which the main procedural processes were established is admirably related by Ralston Hayden in *The Senate and Treaties 1789-1817* (1920). Senator Lodge's views are set out in an important essay in *A Fighting Frigate and Other Essays* (1902). The Department of State published in 1931 an invaluable *List of Treaties submitted to the Senate 1789-1931 which have not gone into force.* There is also an important discussion in E. S. Corwin, *The President's Control of Foreign Relations* (1917).

Senate has interfered with the foreign policy of the
executive, not only by outright rejection of treaties,
but by its exercise of the right to amend them after
long and complicated negotiations, not least in the
case of multilateral instruments. There has been vo-
ciferous complaint of long, and often vexatious, delay.
It is argued that much of the senatorial action is the
outcome, not of defects in the treaties themselves, but
of causes wholly extraneous to them. Sometimes, Senate action has been traced to bitter and, it is argued,
unjustifiable partisanship; the relation of Senator
Lodge to President Wilson over the Versailles Treaty
has been most often cited, in recent years, as the worst
example of such partisanship. Sometimes it is traced
to the determination of the Senate to enhance its prestige in foreign affairs, at the expense of the executive,
and whatever may be the consequences of its action.
Sometimes the relation is blamed on the fact that the
necessity of a two-thirds majority of those voting is
necessary for "approval and consent"; and it is argued
that the result of this requirement is, in fact, to make
a minority of the Senate the masters of the fate of a
proposed treaty. It is urged that, not seldom, the
senators are themselves far less well informed about
the subject matter they decide than those whom they
embarrass by their action; and they yield, it is said,
to all kinds of pressure from interests—personal, national, economic—in reaching a decision.

The whole process is urged as unsatisfactory. It
means that the president of the United States cannot
submit a treaty to the Senate with the certainty either

that, even if it is reasonable, it will be ratified at all, or that it will emerge, if approved, with amendments that are likely to be approved by the other contracting party involved. "The American Constitution," wrote Lord Grey, after his fruitless visit to the United States as ambassador in 1919,[6] "not only makes possible, but, under certain conditions, renders inevitable, a conflict between the executive and the legislature." "I have told you many times," wrote John Hay, in 1898,[7] "that I did not believe another important treaty would ever pass the Senate." It is even argued that the present status of the treaty-making power is a handicap to the influence of the United States in foreign affairs, by reason of the uncertainties it creates, and that the operation of the present mechanism has deprived her of great opportunities that would otherwise have been available.

The critics of the present system have, undoubtedly, a powerful case on their side. But, before we see what truth it contains, it is important to see that case in its proper perspective. The most careful estimate of the statistical aspect of the problem was made by the Department of State in 1935. Of 969 treaties submitted between 1789 and 1934, 682 have been accepted by the Senate; 173 have been amended; 15 have been rejected by it.[8] But, as Professor Dangerfield has shown,[9] of those so amended, the amendments in nearly 59 per cent were insignificant, and in 23 per

[6] London *Times*, January 31, 1920.
[7] W. R. Thayer, *Life of John Hay* (1912), II, 170.
[8] Haynes, *op. cit.*, II, 603.
[9] Dangerfield, *op. cit.*, p. 170.

cent were only moderate in character; vital amendments relate to 18 per cent of the treaties submitted for Senate approval. It is worth noting that, of the treaties submitted, fewer were rejected than the number (53) which, after unconditional approval by the Senate, were never proclaimed by the president.[10] Over 80 per cent of the treaties submitted were ratified within three months, and over 92 per cent were ratified within seven months. Only forty treaties remained without action by the Senate for a period of over a year.[11]

Certain other considerations are important. Many of the proposed extradition treaties, for example, have been amended by the Senate in the light of its persistent refusal to allow extradition to a foreign country for political offenses; in the light of the history of the national composition of the United States, that is a wholly defensible outlook. The famous delay of twenty-one years in the approval of the well-known Isle of Pines Treaty was due to the strong opposition to it of thousands of American citizens who had, under dubious circumstances, been induced to buy land there in the belief that the island would remain under the American flag.[12] Some delay is attributable to the fact that no member of the Senate was particularly interested in securing approval. There are important cases where the president was of one political complexion and the Senate of another. There are

[10] Dangerfield, *op. cit.*, p. 91.
[11] Dangerfield, *op. cit.*, p. 94.
[12] Dangerfield, *op. cit.*, Chap. V.

important cases, the arbitration treaties, for example, where the subject matter was complex and the existence of widely divergent views about the wisdom of approval easily intelligible. There are cases where the maladroit handling by the secretary of state—John Hay is a notable example of this maladroitness—was pivotal in the Senate's attitude. There are cases, further, in which the importance of the subject matter wholly justified either the most scrupulous examination, and therefore delay, and, because of genuine differences about the wisdom of the treaty in the form presented, rejection, or approval only after what Professor Dangerfield calls "vital" reservations. Nor can it be denied that, in many cases, consideration by the Senate has forced the president to further negotiations with the other contracting parties which have resulted in what, from an American angle, is a much more advantageous treaty. And it is at least possible to sympathize with Senator Lodge's insistence that to accept the general arbitration treaties which Mr. Hay had negotiated would have taken from the Senate a power of approval which, rightly or wrongly, was conferred upon it by the Constitution.[13]

It is not, I think, a very powerful argument against the Senate's present power to say that it leaves foreign states in some uncertainty about the outcome of negotiations. It is the business of a foreign state to know the implications of the American Constitution; that is, so to say, a condition precedent to any negotia-

[13] Cf. Haynes, *op. cit.*, p. 616, and the important quotation from the report of the Committee on Foreign Relations in 1911.

tion with the United States. The statistical evidence, moreover, shows that the overwhelming bulk of treaties emerged either wholly unscathed from the ordeal of senatorial examination, or only partially scathed. And it is notable that, Russia apart, "the Senate delays less on those treaties signed with countries with which our diplomatic intercourse is most frequent."[14] For France, Germany, Italy, Great Britain, and Japan, the average is just under eight weeks—not, I think, an excessive period for the detailed examination of the outcome of what is usually prolonged diplomatic interchange.

I am not for a moment denying the force of certain criticisms I propose to consider later. Here I am concerned to note only that those who have attacked the Senate have rarely built their argument on all the facts involved. And account must be taken of the position occupied by the Senate in the constitutional structure of the United States. Rightly or wrongly, the founders associated the Senate with the process of treaty ratification. Whether, as Pierce Butler said,[15] it was their intention that the president should consult the Senate throughout the process of negotiation, it is no longer possible to say. History, in the first instance, and the size of the modern Senate in the second, have made that directness of relation impracticable; it is certainly true that the modern president clings strongly to his prerogative of being the sole effective agent in negotiation. He may consult informally with

[14] Dangerfield, *op. cit.*, p. 102.
[15] Cf. Dangerfield, *op. cit.*, p. 33.

a selected group of senators, especially with the members of the Foreign Relations Committee. He may appoint one or more senators as members of a negotiating commission. He has the means of associating Congress at an early stage with any policy of treaty-making upon which he proposes to embark; as when he asks for an appropriation to meet the expenses of a possible commission and thus obtains implicit approval for the line of action involved. But it is broadly true to say that, in the vast majority of instances, the actual process of negotiation is so wholly executive in character that the Senate is unaware of the results, except in a general way, until the treaty is actually in its hands for consideration.

On any showing, the right of the Senate to examine fully and independently any treaty that comes before it is beyond question. It takes that function seriously; and none of its critics, I presume, would wish this to be otherwise. The real problem lies in the cumbersome nature of the machinery involved, on the one hand; and on the other, in the fact that the very idea of the separation of powers leads each party to the treaty-making process to seek to exalt its own role. This, I think, emerges most fully in the struggle between President Wilson and the Senate over the approval of the Peace of Versailles. It was arrogant folly on the president's part to make the kind of party appeal he did for a Congress that would enable him to make his own kind of peace. It was at least unwise of him to refuse to associate any members of the Senate with the American delegation to the Peace Con-

ference. It was still more unwise to boast that he had
made the kind of treaty which made acceptance of
American association with the League of Nations inevitable of Senate acceptance. In short, the whole
tragic history of the Versailles Treaty was, in the context of the record of the treaty-making power, nothing so much as a wanton defiance of the Senate by
the president which, in the light of the fact that he
had lost his majority there, was certain to be met
with equal defiance.[16] That Senator Lodge, the
leader of the opposition to Mr. Wilson in the Senate,
was moved by the meanest personal considerations
in the excesses to which he allowed himself to go
is, of course, made plain by the amazing letter to
Mr. Henry White he allowed himself to write even
before the Peace Conference began to sit.[17] But, unjustifiable as was the partisanship he displayed, it
is, I suggest, undeniable that there was bitter partisanship, also, on the president's side.

The truth is that the treaty-making power displays
the whole American scheme of government at its
worst. It multiplies all the difficulties that are inherent
in the separation of powers. It provides a channel
for institutional expression to every form of personal
and political antagonism that has developed during
the president's term of office. It heightens the natural
tendency of every legislature to expand its power
at the expense of the executive. None of the expedients
that have been suggested for mitigating its acerbities

[16] Cf. Holt, *op. cit.*, pp. 249-308.
[17] Allan Nevins, *Henry White* (1930), pp. 353-354.

has proved satisfactory. Eleven presidents, for instance, have sought to safeguard themselves from rebuff by asking senatorial advice upon the desirability of entering upon a proposed negotiation.[18] That has had general helpfulness; but it still leaves open the fact that a proposal to negotiate upon a subject is very different from a judgment upon the result of a negotiation. Other presidents have tried to assist themselves either by the means of appointing the proposed agents of negotiation, or by influencing the Senate through appointing its own members as part of the negotiating commission. There is no doubt that this has helped, both to secure approval, and to abridge the delay in securing approval. But it has not solved the central problem. It has avoided the kind of difficulty created by the appointment of executive agents in treaty-making without senatorial consent;[19] but it has not touched the real issue of the substance of the treaty made and the Senate's duty in relation to it.

That central problem has been put in classic terms by Mr. Justice Davis. "In this country," he said,[20] "a treaty is something more than a contract, for the Federal Constitution declares it to be the law of the land. If so, before it can become a law, the Senate in whom rests the power to ratify it, must agree to it. But the Senate are not required to adopt or reject it as

[18] Haynes, *op. cit.*, p. 590.
[19] For a good discussion of these difficulties see Professor H. M. Wriston's admirable book, *Executive Agents in American Foreign Relations* (1929), esp. pp. 237-258, and 292-308.
[20] *Haver v. Yaker* (1869) 9 Wall. 32.

a whole, but may modify it or amend it." There are certain clear advantages in the position. It prevents the legislature from occupying that tragically subordinate position which the House of Commons has come to occupy in foreign affairs. It is a safeguard against the kind of secret diplomacy which characterized Lord Salisbury's bargain with Germany over the Portuguese colonies in Africa, or those of Sir Edward Grey with tsarist Russia over Iran; it is, I think, all to the good that one president cannot bind his successor by the methods of secret diplomacy. It insures a full public discussion of any proposed treaty independently of those who have negotiated it. The very fact, moreover, of the need for the Senate's approval compels the president, in every important instance, to elicit a public opinion upon the desirability of his policy; from this angle, it may be said that the debates in the Senate over the Peace of Versailles probably had an enormous effect in awakening the people of the United States to their responsibilities as a world-power. Lord Harrowby's famous protest that "His Majesty's Government can never acquiesce in the precedent . . . the American government has attempted to establish, of agreeing to ratify such parts of a convention as they may select, and of rejecting other stipulations of it, formally agreed upon by a minister invested with full powers for that purpose,"[21] seems to me to fail because it refuses to realize that it is the precise object of the American Constitution

[21] Hayden, *op. cit.*, pp. 150-152; and see his quotation of Monroe's instructions to the American minister in Sweden in 1816, pp. 208-215.

to prevent a minister from being invested with "full powers" in the sense in which a system like the British understands that term. This has been well put by Senator Lodge. "A British secretary of state for foreign affairs," he wrote,[22] ". . . ought to realize that the Senate can only present its views to a foreign government by formulating them in the shape of amendments which a foreign government may accept, or reject, or meet with counter-propositions, but of which it has no more right to complain than it has to the offer of any germane proposition at any other stage of the negotiation."

In his *Life* of Woodrow Wilson, Mr. Ray Stannard Baker put the case against the present system with exceptional force. "It has been made impossible for America," he wrote,[23] "to speak with a bold and united voice. Nearly every important treaty the country has been called upon to make has become a bone of contention between the executive and the Senate. It is certain that in the years to come, if we are to go forward in the new paths and stand for a clear-cut world policy, we must devise some method of speaking to the world promptly, and with an undivided voice. Our present system leads to utter weakness, muddle and delay; it forces both sides to play politics, and instead of meeting the issue squarely, to indulge in a vast controversy over the prerogatives of two co-ordinate branches of the government. The deadlock between the executive and the Senate every

---

[22] *A Fighting Frigate* (1902), p. 224.
[23] *Woodrow Wilson and the World Settlement* (1922), I, 316.

time we face a really critical foreign problem
tolerable. It not only disgraces us before the n..
but in some future world-crisis may ruin us."

These are strong words; and it is worth while, I
think, to examine them with some particularity. Mr.
Baker, of course, was writing as the official exponent
of Woodrow Wilson's policy, and some allowance
must be made for his natural indignation at its rejection by the Senate. Broadly, it cannot seriously
be said that, on most major matters, the policy of the
United States has lacked a sufficient power to make
itself felt in the politics of world-power. It has applied
the Monroe Doctrine with irresistible force in the
American hemisphere. Its policy of the "open door"
has been a dominating consideration in the politics
of all other powers in the Far East. Its impact on
Europe, as the War of 1914 and its aftermath made
clear, has been continuously profound; no small part,
particularly, of British foreign policy has been moti-
vated by the determination of successive prime ministers to keep in step with American purposes, and any
failure to do so, as the Manchurian affair of 1931-32
made clear, has led to bitter criticism from the opposition. Nor do I think that anyone who examines the
record since Grover Cleveland can doubt that, in
general, the United States has been able to make its
purposes known both "promptly" and with no more
undivided power than any country built upon a system of representative government. There is lacking,
it is true, the swiftness and unity of the dictatorial
powers; but that is precisely because states built upon

the principles of representative government must take account of the reactions of public opinion before their executives act. And Mr. Baker, I assume, would not have it otherwise.

The real pith of his attack lies in his assertion that treaty-making as such invites a controversy between the executive and the legislature. There is substance in this contention, though it must be noted that the invitation is not confined to the treaty-making power only but extends over the whole area of American government. Mr. Baker's argument is really a plea that the Senate should accept a position of inferiority in relation to the president. Upon this view there are two things to be said. First, that the Constitution deliberately provides for equality, and it would, therefore, require a constitutional amendment to attain that end, an amendment unlikely to be secured except after a formidable struggle; and second, that it is asking too much of any legislature to abdicate voluntarily from the exercise of powers upon which a considerable part of its prestige depends. It is worth remembering, moreover, that the Senate has not seldom been as right as the president in its interpretation of what public opinion demanded. Certainly its view of Grant's proposal to take over Santo Domingo, its refusal to accept, in 1868, the purchase of the Danish West Indies, and even its rejection of the Peace of Versailles, may be said to have been in public accord with the sentiment of the time.

Mr. Baker cannot argue that a treaty ought to be confirmed merely because the president has approved

it; presidents have themselves often decided to withdraw treaties that have been proclaimed. It is, too,
worth noting that the power of making executive
agreements not of treaty status—of which the reciprocal agreements of 1882 and 1896 with Mexico are examples[24]—gives any president a wide discretion of
which full advantage has been taken. In a generation,
for example, twenty agreements settling claims of
American citizens for injuries to their property were
made executively, without reference to the approval
of the Senate.[25] The Boxer Protocol of 1901 was so
arranged; as was the well-known exchange of notes
between Mr. Root, as secretary of state, and Baron
Takahira, in 1908; so, despite the discussions it provoked, was the Lansing-Ishii agreement of 1917. None
of these was submitted to the Senate.

Frequently, also, despite Senate hostility, the president has acted as though an agreement had been
made, in matters of grave moment, which was likely
to become a treaty. Theodore Roosevelt has given a
remarkable account in his *Autobiography* of one instance of this attitude on the part of the president.
Speaking of the proposed treaty of 1905 for "the
adjustment of all the Dominican debts, foreign and
domestic," he describes how "I went ahead and administered the proposed treaty anyhow, considering
it as a simple agreement on the part of the executive
which would be converted into a treaty whenever the

[24] Cf. Quincy Wright, *The Control of American Foreign Relations*
(1922), p. 242. As Professor Wright points out, this power has been
amply confirmed by decisions of the Supreme Court.
[25] Haynes, *op. cit.*, p. 643.

Senate acted. After a couple of years, the Senate did act, having previously made some utterly unimportant changes which I ratified and persuaded Santo Domingo to ratify. . . . The Constitution did not explicitly give me power to bring about the necessary agreement with Santo Domingo. But the Constitution did not forbid what I did. I put the agreement into effect, and I continued its execution for two years before the Senate acted, and I would have continued it until the end of my term, if necessary, without any action of Congress."[26] President Tyler acted in a somewhat similar way over the proposed annexation of Texas; and in this case the Senate actually rejected his proposed treaty.[27] "It is evident," as Senator Rayner said in the debate over Mr. Roosevelt's action in Santo Domingo,[28] "that the president under his unquestioned authority to make executive agreements, might go to great lengths, and make arrangements with a foreign power far more serious in character than are often stipulated by formal treaty." He can, in fact, whether by executive agreement or as commander-in-chief, virtually commit the United States to war; and his power to influence congressional action in this regard may easily reduce it to the shadow of its intended substance.

On the evidence, in short, it is ludicrous to represent the president as an embarrassed phantom in the realm of foreign affairs. Roughly, he may be said to be just as strong as the public opinion he is able to

[26] *Autobiography* (1919), pp. 551-552.
[27] *Messages of the Presidents*, IV, 317-318.
[28] Jan. 23, 1906. *Cong. Record*, XL, 1423-1424.

elicit for his policies. The complaints of the critics are, I suggest, largely misplaced, except upon the assumption that the treaty-making power is to be differently exercised than any other part of the Senate's prerogatives. It is important, further, in any assessment of the exercise of this power to remember not only that foreign affairs are more complicated in the twentieth century than they were in the nineteenth, but that the need for popular control in foreign affairs was intended to be one of the features which distinguished the American from other constitutions. It has to be remembered that most of the really important treaties which have been either modified or defeated raised issues of great significance upon which real differences of opinion were, to say the least, permissible. On the arbitration treaties, for example, the Senate's attitude has been shared by important interests in Great Britain; it is notable that the Labor government of Great Britain, in adhering to the optional clause, only did so with far-reaching reservations which deprived the adherence of a good deal of its value; and this was true, also, of British adherence to the Kellogg-Briand pact.

The real target of criticism has been the two-thirds rule. "The irreparable mistake of our Constitution," wrote John Hay,[29] "puts it into the power of one-third + 1 of the Senate to meet with a categorical veto any treaty negotiated by the president, even though it may have the approval of nine-tenths of the people of the nation." There is great weight in this

[29] Letter of August 18, 1899. Thayer, *op. cit.*, II, 219.

view. It helps enormously any group of senators, even an individual, hostile to some treaty upon grounds quite irrelevant to its substance, to organize opposition to it with some hope that it may be successful. This senator is opposed to the treaty because he dislikes the state with which it is being made; that senator hopes, by his opposition, to please a strong religious or national element in his constituency; another may feel that opposition involves the duty of preventing any success being accredited to the president of the other party; another, again, may be on bad terms with the president of his own party and use this means of expressing the fact. Yet even this criticism may be pushed too far. The subject matter of most treaties does not easily lead to popularity for the senator opposing it; except upon the largest issues it is doubtful whether such opposition arouses any widespread interest at all. I doubt, for instance, whether there is any evidence that a senator's attitude on the convention of 1883 (which was rejected for lack of a two-thirds majority) with Mexico for the retrying of claims created any strong feeling about him among the people of the United States. And it has been shown that of all the treaties submitted to the Senate, none failed of approval because of the two-thirds vote before 1860, and only twelve between that date and 1935.[30] Of the twelve it is difficult, says Professor Fleming, to regard more than two of serious importance, even though he thinks that the passage of the

[30] Haynes, *op. cit.*, II, 659.

others "would have notably improved our relations with a foreign state."[31]

The case against the two-thirds rule is, however, a substantial one on another ground. It is important because of what may be termed its prenatal effects. The knowledge that a little bloc of recalcitrant senators may hold up or modify a wise proposal has adverse effect both upon the prospect of embarking upon it and upon the process of negotiation itself. This has been well put by Mr. De Witt Clinton Poole, himself an American diplomat of long experience. "The record," he writes,[32] "does not show from what wise measures the president or his secretary has been estopped by perhaps unfounded fear of what a few senators may do, nor is it demonstrable into what brusque and harmful actions the spectre on Capitol Hill has frightened them. In the light of my own reading and my own experience in Washington, I am confident that both misfortunes have frequently befallen." No one, I think, can read the correspondence and diaries of presidents and secretaries of state without the sense that this is largely true. Anyone who reads, to take the supreme instance only, the detailed story of President Wilson's negotiations at Versailles can hardly avoid the conclusion that at each stage of his activities the shadow of Senator Lodge dogged his footsteps like an evil fate, and was not without responsibility for many of Wilson's blunders both before and after the treaty was made.

[31] *The Treaty Veto of the American Senate*, p. 304.
[32] Haynes, *op. cit.*, p. 661.

The case, therefore, for a revision of the two-thirds rule is, I think, a clear one. Before we consider possible alternatives, however, there is one general remark that it is worth while to make. No critic of the present form of the treaty-making power suggests its confinement to the hand of the executive alone. In the light both of American and of foreign experience I think this is wise. A self-willed president of dominant personality, Tyler, for instance, or Polk, or Theodore Roosevelt, or Woodrow Wilson, might easily have taken the United States into dubious foreign adventures for which public opinion was unprepared, for which, also, there would have been little justification, had it not been for the knowledge that the Senate would ultimately review the results of their activities. "The spectre on Capitol Hill" may have frightened them into many "brusque and harmful actions"; it is, I think, equally unquestionable that it has frightened them out of many they might otherwise have attempted. A president eager for imperialist adventure, or concerned to exercise influence in Europe in a particular direction, might easily, in the absence of Senate control, be a source of grave danger to the American people. And this view is, I suggest, reinforced by experience of systems like that of Great Britain where the control of foreign affairs is, in fact, "executive altogether." For the only real control of the House of Commons is of a *post-mortem* nature. It is presented by the cabinet with a *fait accompli*, rejection of which involves the defeat of the government and a subsequent general election.

There is no instance in modern times where the government has had an assured majority, upon which its supporters have been willing to take that risk. The result is that the executive in Great Britain has a primacy in foreign affairs so assured that, save where a leakage gives public opinion—as in the Hoare-Laval incident—an unexpected knowledge of events, it has little reason to trouble itself about the impact of foreign affairs upon the House of Commons. The only real limit to its powers is the decision exercised by the voters at a subsequent general election; and that decision, as in the case of the doctrine of nonintervention in Spain, or the sacrifice of Czecho-Slovakia at Munich in 1938, may come too late to affect the results of the government's policy.

What, therefore, is in dispute in the United States is not the desirability of legislative control which, in some form, is conceded by all the critics; it is the narrower question of the method by which that legislative control should be secured. Some suggest that a simple majority of the Senate should suffice for the confirmation of a treaty; others suggest that the House of Representatives should be joined with the treaty-making power and that, as with a declaration of war, a majority in both houses should suffice for confirmation. This, it is interesting to note, was the method proposed by James Wilson in the constitutional convention, though only Pennsylvania voted for its adoption there; and it has recently been approved by an eminent Democratic candidate for the presidency, who has also had ambassadorial experience, Mr. John W. Davis.[33] It has been suggested that, for the purpose of confirmation, both houses might meet as a single assembly; and Mr. S. W. McCall, at one time a well-known congressman, has urged that the treaty-making power should be transferred wholly to the House of Representatives on the ground that its frequency of re-election brings it nearer than the Senate can ever hope to be to whatever public opinion is upon issues of foreign policy.[34] Professor Dangerfield, at the close of his illuminating and elaborate examination of the treaty-making powers, will have none of these proposals. He suggests the creation of a special Foreign Relations Cabinet to consist of "the secretary of state, the under-secretary of state, a senior drafting officer, the chairman and the ranking minority members of the Senate Committee on Foreign Relations and the House Committee on Foreign Affairs." " Such a cabinet," he writes,[35] "would combine the experts of the Department, and the political leaders of both houses who deal with foreign affairs."

Of these proposals, the most logical is obviously the transference of the treaty-making power to a majority of both houses of Congress. This homologates the peace-making control of foreign policy with that involved in the making of war; and it has the further advantage, which is important, of associating with

[33] Haynes, op. cit., p. 661. Mr. W. J. Bryan and Colonel House were also in favor of this method.

[34] Atlantic Monthly (Sept. 1920), p. 395. I have been unable to find any other supporter of Mr. McCall's proposal.

[35] Dangerfield, op. cit., p. 321. Professor Dangerfield points out that this proposal was first made by Professor Quincy Wright in his Control of Foreign Relations, p. 371.

treaty-making that branch of the legislature which has to implement any appropriations necessary for treaty fulfilment. I do not think it is a serious objection that the House is now a large body; the Senate itself has never been small enough to act as a presidential council. It is, of course, a difficulty that the House may be of a different political complexion from that of the Senate, and that this may, in important instances, lead to a deadlock; but since the same situation already exists as between the Senate and the president, I do not think this can be regarded as an insuperable objection. It may be, as Mr. Hayden has noted,[36] that the method "abandons all attempt at secrecy, and would subject the treaty to amendment or reservation by both branches of Congress, with adjustments by compromise in conference committee." But this, in any case, is an experience with which the president is familiar, and it raises no obstacle that is not inherent in the ordinary legislative process of the United States. It is a better proposal, I think, than that of simply abolishing the two-thirds rule in the Senate for several reasons. Both houses are concerned in foreign affairs; it is therefore appropriate that both should have an equal relevance to them. And where a bicameral system based on popular election exists, it is illogical to exclude one chamber from direct concern with a fundamental branch of policy. The proximity, moreover, of the House of Representatives to election would render it valuably accessible to public

[36] Hayden, *op. cit.*, II, 661.

opinion in those issues upon which—they are rare—
a strong public opinion can be formed.

I do not think there is much to be said for Professor Dangerfield's scheme. It divides executive authority and responsibility where it is least desirable to divide it—at the place where initiative must be taken and the process of negotiation begun. It jeopardizes secrecy and dispatch, especially in those periods where Congress is not in session. It raises grave difficulties for the president in every instance where the Congress, or one house of it, happens not to be of his political complexion. It would make his own relations to his secretary of state no easy matter; and it might easily divide the latter's allegiance between the president and the two chairmen, as well as the ranking minority members, of the respective congressional committees. It is, no doubt, true that where the Congress members of such a cabinet supported the treaty, they would be able to recommend it in Congress with more *expertise* than at present; but it is, on the other hand, also obvious that, where they opposed it, the passage of the treaty would thereby be rendered more difficult. The evidence Professor Dangerfield has himself so illuminatingly collected suggests that, though the strong support of the chairman of the Foreign Relations Committee of the Senate may be helpful in securing the rapid consideration of a treaty, it is very far from being decisive where confirmation is concerned. Most of the advantages urged by Professor Dangerfield for his proposal are already open to the president in other ways; and one who, like McKinley, has shown that he is skilful in handling the Senate, can obviously take full advantage of them. The dangers of the proposal seem to me to outweigh its advantages. It multiplies the present prospect of legislative encroachment upon the president's power, especially in the twilight zone of executive agreements and in that complicated area involved in his functions as commander-in-chief. It hampers his initiative, especially where he is dealing with a Congress dominated by the opposition party. It offers, also, it is worth adding, manifold opportunities for the kind of action Senator Lodge thought fit to make in the prelude to the Peace Conference of Versailles.

A foreigner may consider the alternatives; it is, happily, an American task to decide between them. I am satisfied to point out that, in my own judgment, the case against the Senate has been enormously overestimated. I do not for a moment deny that an inherent jealousy of the executive, purely partisan objections, and even personal spite, have entered into the senatorial exercise of its power. Weighing all these, I still think that, somewhere in the legislature of the United States, a power of this kind should, in the face of all its difficulties, be lodged. Despite its extent, the authority of the president in foreign affairs remains immense; he is, on any showing, the motive-power of the whole system. It has one great result which is not attained in anything like a proportionate degree in other systems, and, most notably, not attained in the British system: it enforces upon the president the obligation to give reasons for what he is doing. He is compelled to educate public opinion; he cannot drive it. There is the assurance—of immense importance in representative government—that the case against what he is doing will not only be fully stated, but that, at each stage of his activities, he will be forced to take account of that case. Not seldom, in the conflicts that have arisen, the Senate has been perverse and mistaken; but, not seldom also, the president has been perverse and mistaken too. The system leaves room, as room should be left, for wide presidential initiative; but, very wisely I think, it makes the success of that initiative largely dependent upon the power of the president to maintain his hold upon public opinion. In a democracy, I think it is right that this should be the case. An Englishman, to take a concrete case, may well regret, in the light of its aftermath, the Senate's rejection of the Peace of Versailles. But anyone who compares the process of its ratification in the Senate, on the one hand, and in the House of Commons, on the other, can hardly help concluding that, if there is to be democracy in foreign affairs, the principle which underlies the American system is by far superior to the principle which underlies the British. I cannot, further, avoid the opinion that the large superiority in the reporting of foreign news in the American press, as compared with the British, is not unconnected with the fact that the basic principle of control is in the one case democratic, while in the other it is aristocratic. It is not insignificant, in the postwar years, that much discussion has been devoted in Great Britain to the problem of democratizing the control of foreign policy. I would not, for a moment, say that the problem has been solved in the United States. But it is, I think, beyond doubt that the American safeguards against executive unwisdom —I use a neutral word—are an improvement of profound importance upon anything that Europe has so far evolved.

3

I turn to a very different, if connected, aspect of the president's relation with the Senate. That body shares with him the nominating power. He has the sole right to submit names for its approbation; but the Senate is wholly free to confirm or to reject the choice he makes. The idea of the founders was, no doubt, to prevent the president from building up an unbreakable executive power. It was assumed that the merit of the proposed appointee would be the one issue with which the Senate would concern itself. "It could hardly happen," wrote Alexander Hamilton,[37] "that the majority of the Senate would feel any other complacency towards the object of an appointment than such as the appearances of merit might inspire, and the proofs of the want of it destroy."

Rarely has the failure of a prophecy by a great man been more complete. From the beginning of Washington's administration, the Senate's share in the power of appointment has been, in its essence, exercised in

[37] *The Federalist*, No. 66.

part for party purposes, and in part on personal grounds. The senatorial veto on appointments begins with the foundation of the republic, and by the time, at any rate, of Andrew Jackson the system so gracefully called "senatorial courtesy" was well established. It has been happily defined by Professor Lindsay Rogers. "Senatorial courtesy," he writes,[38] "is a kind of 'liberum veto,' and means no more than this: that while the Senate will not suggest particular nominations, it expects that the president, in naming certain local office-holders (e.g., postmasters and collectors of the customs), will choose persons satisfactory to the senator or senators of the president's political party from the state in which the offices are located, or from which the appointees come. 'The strength of the pack is the wolf, and the strength of the wolf is the pack'; consequently, if senators are ignored, or if their objections are flouted, the Senate in most cases will not approve the nominations. It is difficult to speak with decision about a scheme of appointment the range of which is constantly changing. But it is not, I think, an exaggeration to say that, nowadays, the Senate has a contingent veto power over something like 18,000 appointments."

Some of them it will usually accept without question. It is customary to agree to the president's choice of his cabinet; though this has not always been the case. Madison was compelled to withdraw the name of Gallatin for the post of secretary of state merely because Senator Smith had a brother for whom he

[38] Lindsay Rogers, *The American Senate* (1926), p. 25.

coveted the place;[39] and I have already referred to the rejection of Mr. Coolidge's nomination—on quite intelligible grounds—of Charles B. Warren as his attorney-general. But, as a rule, the Senate realizes that where cabinet posts are in question it is desirable for the president to have his own way; after all, he knows best the team with which he can live. Much the same is true of ambassadors, though even here objection has been taken to appointments in an indefensible way; the rejection of Gallatin as ambassador to Russia, of Van Buren, who resigned the secretaryship of state to go to London, of Norman Hapgood, who had been nominated to Denmark by President Wilson, are all cases of this kind. Yet, again, proportionately speaking the Senate has not been too ungenerous, perhaps on occasion even excessively gracious, to presidential nominations to diplomatic posts.

It is in the other realms of appointment that the exercise of this power is seen at its worst. It has both a negative and a positive side. On the negative side, the worst type of rejection is that in which a senator bases his opposition merely on the ground that the proposed appointee is "personally obnoxious" to him. Senator Gallinger, of New Hampshire, after a struggle lasting over two years, prevented the nomination of a distinguished lawyer, Mr. George Rublee, to the Federal Trade Commission solely on this basis.[40] Senator Hoar has given us an account of a nomination

[39] Henry Adams, *The Life of Albert Gallatin* (1879), p. 391.
[40] Cf. *New Republic*, May 20, 1916.

by President Grant made under circumstances so dubious that it may well have been the cause of Grant's failure to secure a third term.[41] The famous struggle over the collectorship of the Port of New York between Garfield and Roscoe Conkling is well known. And we have been told by Polk of the amazing nonchalance with which senatorial recommendations are too often made to the president, which he has rarely any alternative but to accept. The power is exercised ruthlessly right up to nominations for the Supreme Court. Between 1789 and 1938 the Senate has been responsible for the withdrawal of 21 nominations out of 109 submitted to it—practically 20 per cent.[42]

It is impossible, of course, to doubt that there have been occasions when the power of veto has been wisely used. Bad presidential nominations are not, alas, rare; and Senate debates like those on the appointment of Mr. Hughes as chief justice of the United States—he was confirmed by 52 votes to 26—or that as a result of which the nomination of Judge Parker to the Court was rejected, serve a useful purpose in reminding the president of the importance of remembering the qualities for which he ought to look in an appointee to the bench. But, frankly, it is the exception rather than the rule for the Senate, even in the case of the Supreme Court, to make an impersonal assessment of qualifications. The important things are the purchase of support by the presi-

[41] Hoar, *op. cit.,* I, 212.
[42] Warren, *The Supreme Court in United States History* (1922), Vol. III, Appendix.

dent from among his own party, and the effort of the
senator to see that his relation to the distribution of
patronage is effective in consolidating his own position in the political life of the state. The misery
through which a president must pass in effecting that
distribution must be seen to be believed. He may,
like Theodore Roosevelt, take high ground about the
standards he proposes to maintain;[43] experience of the
actual operation of the power will rapidly bring him
down to lower levels.

I do not myself think that the problem the issue
presents is at all an easy one. There can be no sort
of doubt but that the Senate, especially in relation to
the practice of "courtesy" has gravely abused its
power. But there can be little doubt that, left unim-
peded by the prospect of a senatorial veto, the president's abuse of his patronage would be equally grave.
As the system stands at present, it is, I think, fair
to say that public opinion will compel some real degree of judicial-mindedness in the case of appointments to the Supreme Court and certain commissions
like that on interstate commerce and the tariff; this is
not necessarily the case, but there is at least a probability that it will be so because there is likely to be a
special public interested in, and watchful of, the
quality and fitness of the men who are chosen to fill
them. Once, however, we leave those posts on which
the eyes of the nation are fixed, the whole patronage
system is bedeviled by mean and sordid interests com-

[43] J. B. Bishop, *Theodore Roosevelt* (1920), I, 157, and cf. pp. 235,
248, 442.

peting for the party and personal advantages that can be secured by its exercise.

The obvious thing for an Englishman to say is that before the reforms of 1870 the patronage system in Great Britain was also mean and sordid; that, with the coming of the merit system, a wholly different character has been given to political appointments, and that the United States can end this problem by the simple method of replacing the spoils system by the merit system. I do not think the problem is as simple as this suggests. Political parties are real and obstinate things which have to be kept alive. In Great Britain we have largely—not wholly—removed the virus of patronage from the world of the civil service. But we have replaced it, so far as rewarding political service is concerned, by an immense extension of the system of political "honors," in which even appointment to the office of justice of the peace has become, in the overwhelming number of cases, a reward for party service. To some extent this is true, also, of appointments to the High Court;[44] and it obtains in relation to a small, but important, number of colonial governorships. And hardly a royal commission is nominated but some of the appointments to which are explicable only by the desire of the prime minister or his cabinet colleague to reward a political friend. With the growth, too, of public corporations like the British Broadcasting Corporation and the London Passenger Transport Board, there has been, in recent years, a significant increase in the paid patronage at the government's dis-

[44] Cf. my *Studies in Law and Politics* (1932), Chap. 7.

posal; and it is well known that directorships on the board of the Suez Canal Company—as well paid a sinecure as there is in the disposal of the British government—have always been used to reward the higher forms of political service.

Nominations to a title, of course, are not open to the president by the fiat of the Constitution; and a political party without this source of reward would find itself in a difficult position. There can be no doubt that much of the work which, in Great Britain, is held worthy of a peerage or a knighthood, is, in the United States, rewarded with an ambassadorship or the lucrative collectorship of a great customs port. To abolish this system would be to dig deep into the foundations of party politics. The disturbance to the national and to local political machines would be immense, and it is by no means easy to predict the consequences that would follow. It is not enough, I think, merely to say that the patronage system must end. Is it to end on the senatorial side, or the presidential, or both? For let us clearly recognize that it is an evil for which both sides are equally responsible. Since Jackson's time, at any rate, no president has had any compunction in using his power of patronage to get the support he wanted in Congress, and at least since then there have been few senators who have failed to use the influence the power of confirmation brings with it to assure their position in their constituencies. To make the whole system of appointment one based, like the British system, wholly on merit, might easily have two dangerous consequences. On the one hand, it might easily jeopardize the president's power to force through necessary or useful measures by depriving him of one of the most important sanctions of that power he now possesses. On the other, it might throw members of Congress, and especially members of the Senate, into a far greater dependence upon rich men and important interests, like the railroads and the public utilities, than is now the case. Neither, I think, would be a desirable result.

Of one thing, certainly, I am sure. It would be a great mistake to abolish the power of the Senate over appointments, leaving the president the free hand he would then possess. For it is a power so obviously capable of abuse, above all in the hands of a weak man, that it would be certain to be indefensibly administered. You have only to remember the use to which Grant and Harding, even with the present safeguards, were prepared to put that power to see that this is the case. I do not suppose for a moment that it would enable any president to build up an unbeatable machine of officeholders. But it would offer temptations of grave proportions to corrupt interests to secure the staffing of the courts and the great commissions with men willing to exchange favors in return for appointments to place. Anyone who thinks, for example, of a Securities and Exchange Commission staffed by the creatures of Wall Street; or of a National Labor Relations Board whose members shared the ideals of the National Association of Manufacturers; or of an Interstate Commerce Commission incapable of detachment upon the thorny problems of railroad rates and railroad consolidations; can at once see the dangerous vistas that are conjured up. The Senate has made its mistakes, and its sins, in the context of the appointing power, are manifold. But it has always contained a number of men, of whom the late Senator La Follette was outstanding in the last generation, and Senator Norris in our own, who have been the unpurchasable and relentless guardians of the public interest in appointments; who have played, in short, the part that Hamilton assumed the Senate as a whole would play. It is a pity that there have not been more of such men. But, so long as such men are there, they act as watchdogs of the public in a way for which, granted the president's power, nothing could compensate if it were abolished.

I believe, therefore, that so long as the president's unfettered power to nominate over the present wide range of personnel remains, so long also, with all its faults, the Senate's power of approval must remain. I confess that I should like to see the range of the power limited to proportions more akin to British practice. I think the United States, in the long run, has everything to gain and little to lose by removing as much as possible of its administrative personnel from the grip of the spoils system. But it must, on any realistic consideration, be admitted that this raises two grave problems. On the one hand, there is the issue of what compensating means the president is to have to retain his hold on Congress. On the other, there is the very difficult problem of how far precisely the limitation on his power to appoint is to go.

The first problem goes down to the root of the American scheme of government. It is not enough to say that the president will still be able to appeal to public opinion, and that where he is right he will be victorious. This is to omit both the time factor and the power of propaganda in the modern world. Granted the separation of powers, I do not see that there can be any doubt that the less the president has to offer for the votes he receives, the less will be his authority in the legislature, the weaker, accordingly, will be the pressure of leadership he can exert. Let us remember that, at best, his leadership of the party is a fleeting phenomenon; that he is dealing with innumerable local machines that are, at best, only partially responsive to his control; that he has no such sanction at his disposal as the threat of dissolution; that party discipline in the United States is, by reason of the separation of powers, much less rigid than it is in the European countries; and it becomes clear that every serious deprivation of powers he may suffer is almost an invitation to Congress to move to usurpation in a sphere that should properly be his. My friend Professor Brogan, in his remarkable book,[45] has urged at once the abolition of the senatorial power over appointment and the extension of the president's authority. I agree that this would be achieved if the spoils system remained, and if the disposal of the system were to be solely a presidential prerogative. But if the spoils system, as a principle, is to go—and the case against it is really unanswerable—then the presi-

45 *Government of the People* (1933), p. 382.

dent's position would be far weaker than it is today. For reasons I have already indicated, I do not believe the United States, at this period of its history, can afford weak presidents. The dilemma thus presented is one that goes to the heart of the whole scheme of American institutions; and I shall try to assess its significance at the end of this book.

The second problem is, of course, a much narrower one; but its importance can easily be overlooked. The British system of appointment has, in the last seventy years, succeeded in creating an administrative personnel of high quality and great influence. It has freed both the cabinet and members of Parliament from all the nauseating habits of a patronage system. But it has brought in its train serious problems of its own. It has, it is true, given the British people a civil service unsurpassed in independence and courage. But it has also, in recent years particularly, raised the question whether the price that has been paid is not an absence of the spirit of invention, a want of imagination in seeing the need to open out new lines of state policy, which are of increasing importance. "It is one business to do what must be done," wrote Sir Henry Taylor,[46] "another to devise what ought to be done. It is in the spirit of the British government, as hitherto existing, to transact only the former business." I think that is still largely true. Where large-scale innovation has been attempted the impulse to it has usually been communicated from outside, and there have been too many occasions when its introduction has been, ably

[46] *The Statesman* (ed. of 1924), p. 113.

and pertinaciously—because civil servants at the top of their departments are able and pertinacious men —resisted from within. The tradition of a civil service like that of Great Britain is to maximize the avoidance of blunders rather than to take the risks, with the dangers of mistake, for which the future seems to call. In general, a British civil servant gets to a really influential position in his department after some twenty years' service. By that time he has been habituated to a routine of thought which deprecates large-scale departure from the traditions to which he is accustomed. It requires a minister of very notable capacity to make headway against such an habituation. I suspect that the British civil service is very nearly the perfect instrument for the negative state. I think it has yet to be proved that it is, in its present form, adequate for the positive state, particularly for a positive state which requires immense administrative experimentalism if it is to adapt itself to a rapidly changing, perhaps to a revolutionary world.[47]

Something of this problem would inevitably confront an American president if his power over patronage were as largely abolished as that power has been abolished in Great Britain. Allowances would have to be made for its existence. A performing president would have to be sure not only that he could count upon the necessary support from the bureaucracy, but also of the necessary inventiveness and risk-taking. Is a stable civil service of the British kind compatible with these qualities? My answer is that we do not yet

[47] Cf. my *Parliamentary Government in England* (1938), Chap. 6.

know; and I think it worth while to record my own impression, based, I may venture to add, upon considerable investigation, that there has been more of these two vital qualities in Washington under Franklin Roosevelt than there has been in Whitehall for something like a generation. I do not deny that Whitehall produces these men—Sir Robert Morant, for example;[48] but when they emerge, they stand out like Mount Rainier amidst the surrounding range. I am satisfied to make it as clear as I can that any effort to deal with the ramifications of the civil service problem in the United States must at least bear these considerations in mind. On the one hand, to end the spoils system is to risk the pervasiveness of the president's influence over the Congress; on the other, to provide him with a permanent civil service on the British model may well deprive him of the human instrumentalities he requires for large-scale change. The problem is of the proportions that call for the qualities of a Bentham. No one who speculates upon its implications can avoid seeing how they reach far into the foundations of the American commonwealth. It is in the degree that this is realized that it has the prospect of being met with prescience and imagination.

4

The Senate has a clear power over appointments; it has a less well-defined relation to removals from

[48] Cf. B. Allen, *Sir Robert Morant* (1934), and the last chapter of Sir George Newman's *A Century of Public Health* (1939).

office. That the consent of the Senate to removals would be necessary, Hamilton did not doubt;[49] but Madison took a very different view. "If you say that a bad man in office," he wrote,[50] "shall not be displaced but by and with the advice and consent of the Senate, the president is no longer answerable for the conduct of the officer; all will depend upon the Senate. You hereby destroy a real responsibility without obtaining even the shadows." From the outset of the republic grave fears have been expressed if the president were to have an uncontrolled power of removal; though there was little in the record of the early presidents to justify such a fear and, in a considerable degree, as Professor Thach has pointed out, it is implicit in the general nature of executive power.[51]

The first great clash came under President Jackson; and from that time onward, especially under President Johnson, the fires of controversy have waxed and waned. Cases like the removal of Duane, the secretary of the treasury, by Jackson, and the suspension of Stanton, the secretary of war, by Johnson, show the profundity of the authority claimed by the president; while senatorial pressure to remove high officials, Gouverneur Morris, for instance, as minister to France, and Denby, as secretary of the navy under Coolidge, are instances of the struggle for effective control of this prerogative on the other side. A further problem arises as to the creation of offices. May Congress, in its wisdom, attach such conditions to

[49] *The Federalist*, No. 77.
[50] Speech in the House of Representatives, May 19, 1789.
[51] *The Creation of the Presidency* (1922), p. 159.

the creation of posts as to render a dismissal dependent upon its consent? In *Myers* v. *U. S.*[52] the Supreme Court, by a majority, held that the denial of an unrestricted power of removal to the president is unconstitutional; though, on that occasion, both Mr. Justice Brandeis and Mr. Justice Holmes held that Congress was entitled to place what limitations on removal it pleased. But in *Humphrey's Executor* v. *U. S.*[53] the Court seems to have narrowed the area covered by the earlier decision and to have argued that where the post involved is not purely "executive," and concerns a removal from an "independent agency" like the Interstate Commerce Commission or the Federal Reserve Board, the Congress has the right to lay down conditions within which the president may act in removal, and that a removal outside these conditions would be illegal. There is a clear area of difficulty between the two cases; and it cannot yet be said, I think, that the legal position has been settled.

My own view is that, so far as removals are concerned, there are two divisions of the problem to which different considerations apply. On the one hand, there are the ordinary executive agencies of the government. There, as I think, the president's right to be unfettered in his discretion is unquestionable. His duty is the "faithful execution of the laws"; he is entitled to the instruments he deems suitable to that execution. He may make mistakes; he may act in a partisan way; he may, as the Senate has so often feared,

[52] (1926), 272 U. S. 52.
[53] (1935), 295 U. S. 602.

seek to use his authority to build up a personal machine. But it is difficult to see what any president will, in this realm, really gain by an unwise exercise of his discretion. Wherever he dismisses an official, he has to make a new appointment; and there is reason and to spare for supposing that the Senate will interpose its veto, as it did upon Roger Taney after the dismissal of Duane, whenever it thinks the presidential exercise has been unwarranted. So long as the official involved is carrying out a function for the proper exercise of which the president is ultimately responsible, I cannot see that interference with that responsibility is desirable. In any political system, there is a point at which trust must be placed somewhere. It is of the essence of the American scheme that, for the executive process, trust should be placed in the president. It seems to me to follow from this that legislative interference with discretion in that trust is, if it reaches the point of prohibition, wholly undesirable.

I do not mean, thereby, that Congress should be estopped from the expression of its opinion. Action like that taken in the Denby case seems to me wholly undesirable.[54] That is an expression of opinion upon which the president is free to act or to refrain from acting, as he pleases, though at his peril. In a way, a resolution such as was passed in the Denby case is like a vote of "no confidence" in a particular minister in the House of Commons. It does not, indeed, force the ministry out, as it would do in Great Britain. But

---

[54] For a good account of the Denby case see Haynes, *op. cit.*, II, 816 f.

it serves the wholly admirable purpose of informing
the president, and beyond him the people of the
United States, that grave matters are afoot, of which
the legislature takes a serious view. I do not think
such resolutions should be passed save in cases of
exceptional momentousness. But the Denby case was
such a one. Here, after all, was a cabinet minister
at the least culpably negligent in an affair which led
to the criminal prosecution of two of his colleagues,
and the conviction of one of them. To argue, as
Senator Borah did, that Congress has no right under
the Constitution to pass such a resolution because the
dismissal of a cabinet officer is not within its power
(save through the formal and unlikely process of im-
peachment) is to take far too narrow a view of the
legislative function. Criticism of the administration
is inherent in that function, is, indeed, one of the
most valuable services it can perform. To hinder its
performance upon formal grounds is as harmful to
the president himself as it may be to the interests it is
his duty to serve.

But the judges apart (and they are separately provided for under the Constitution)[55] it seems to me
clear, also, that there is a type of governmental post
in which, by its very nature, there ought to be safeguards against an unlimited presidential discretion to
remove. There are posts, of which the Interstate Commerce Commission is the outstanding example, the
holders of which are intended to have a quasi-judicial
position, or which involve the passing upon problems

[55] Art. III, Sec. 1.

that are not intended to be dealt with along the ordinary lines of the party battle. Here, I suggest, it is impossible to doubt that Congress both could and should prescribe the terms upon which removals from office may be made; and of such a post as that of the comptroller-general of the United States, it seems to me obvious that accountability to Congress rather than to the president is desirable.[56] Sometimes the congressional desire to secure independence from the passing policy of the government of the day has been attempted by a deliberate demand for a bipartisan structure of the agency concerned. Where a president has sought to get round the statutory provision, as Mr. Coolidge did with Mr. D. J. Lewis, by asking for an "undated letter of resignation as the price for sending the reappointment to the Senate,"[57] his action seems to me wholly unjustifiable. A great deal of modern administration is of a quasi-judicial nature the quality of which depends upon public faith in the maximum possible impartiality of the administrators. That Congress should be entitled, in such cases, legislatively to safeguard as much of that impartiality as it can is, I think, beyond dispute. President Franklin Roosevelt, for example, wrote to Mr. Humphrey, of the Tariff Commission, requesting his resignation on the ground that "the aims and purposes of the Commission can be carried out most effectively with per-

[56] On posts of this character see the admirable remarks of Professor Lindsay Rogers, *op. cit.*, pp. 45 f. His book contains also (pp. 257-270) a valuable list of statutes restricting the power of the president to appoint or remove.

[57] Rogers, *op. cit.*, p. 47.

sonnel of my own selection"; while, at the same time, he seems to have been wholly satisfied with the quality of Mr. Humphrey's work. The statute creating the commission lays it down[58] that removals shall be for "inefficiency, neglect of duty, or malfeasance in office." Since Mr. Humphrey was charged with none of these, it is difficult to see on what legitimate grounds he could have been asked to resign.

The case of Mr. Humphrey is clearly distinguishable from that of Dr. A. E. Morgan, at the time of his removal the chairman of the Board of the Tennessee Valley Authority.[59] Here, there was definite evidence upon which the president was entitled to find that the attitude of Dr. Morgan to his colleagues made impossible the proper fulfilment of the authority's function. The president held, personally, "hearings," in which all the evidence necessary for a judgment was before him. His decision was, no doubt, an act of "discretion"; but it was one which an average reasonable man was likely, in the circumstances, to find appropriate to the facts involved. This type of case, though it gave rise to a passionate debate in Congress, was clearly of a different order from that of Humphrey. In the latter's case, there were no charges against the official. The president seems merely to have felt that he would be more satisfied with an administrative body composed of his own nominees. But since the very nature of the statute

[58] 39 U. S. Stat. 795. S. 700.
[59] For a full account of this case see the account of the president's meetings with Dr. Morgan, together with the opinion of the solicitor-general, in his message to Congress of March 23, 1938.

under which the commission operated was intended to prevent the president from having a discretion of this kind, I cannot see any possible answer to the judgment of the Supreme Court—unanimously affirmed—that he did not possess it.

For, in cases of the Humphrey type, the object of legislation is to offer the citizen a guarantee that the official is independent of the political executive in the view he forms upon its policies. It is as legitimate to safeguard that guarantee as it is to secure the tenure of a judge from executive interference. I agree that, where a vacancy occurs, the president is entitled, once he pays due regard to whatever statutory qualifications may be exacted, to put forward men of his own way of thought rather than of that opposed to him. Such officials, like, indeed, members of the Supreme Court themselves, are in that twilight area where the facts have to be seen from an angle that, so far as is humanly possible, transcends the individual limitations of judgment. Just as a justice of the Supreme Court ought not to find a statute unconstitutional just because he thinks it unwise, so a member of one of these quasi-independent agencies ought not to stand against a presidential policy because he dislikes it. The question, for him, is whether the presidential line of policy is likely to frustrate the purpose of the agency upon which he serves, and no more; he ought, even, to lean toward that line if it has serious pretensions to "reasonableness." For administration becomes an impossible task if, within the confines of the executive power, agencies exist the end of which is, if possible, to strike into impotence the policy the administration is seeking to pursue. That task is essentially a legislative one; and, within the safeguards I have suggested, the larger the leeway that is given to the president the better. I do not doubt that this freedom may be abused or badly handled. But the correction of such errors is a task which devolves upon Congress. The answer to a bad administrative policy is, its legality apart, not a matter during the president's term of office for officials of his government; the answer is in the legislature which is elected for precisely that end. And if the legislature is incapable of performing that task of correction, it is a function which devolves upon the people. Any other policy than this destroys, I am confident, the foundations of effective government.

V

CONCLUDING OBSERVATIONS

I

THE president of the United States is elected by a method which now bears no relation to the purpose it is intended to fulfil. A majority in the electoral college may defeat a majority in the nation. It did so in 1876 and in 1888; it nearly did so in 1884 and in 1916. From any angle the electoral college is an anachronism, and the choice by states is undesirable. It has a real effect on the choice of candidates. Because, in all normal circumstances, the attitude of a particular state is known, the tendency is encouraged in parties not merely to select the candidate from a doubtful state, but also to make "deals" before the election with the machines of particular states, with a view to securing the nomination and the victory of a particular candidate. The Democratic party is confident that it will win the South; and it has tended, therefore, since the Civil War, to take its presidential candidate from the Eastern seaboard and particularly from New York. The Northeast is predominantly Republican; but the Republicans can win an election only by carrying all the states of the Middle West, and those on the border between the North and South. They have, therefore, sought for candidates in the middle western states in order to achieve this alliance. "Statesmanship in this nation," wrote F. J. Turner,[1] "consists not only in representing the special interests of the leader's own section, but in finding a formula that will bring the different regions together in a common policy."

It is easy to show how much of American politics has been bedeviled, in the context of the presidency, by the search for this formula. Jefferson and Jackson owed their victories to their success in finding it, as Clay and Calhoun owed their defeats to a failure in the same pursuit. The failure of Negro suffrage in the South has been the graveyard of Republican representation there; and both in the emphasis of issues, and in the choice of candidates, it is the inherent implication of sectionalism to which fundamental attention must be paid. I think, therefore, that once it is agreed that the transcendence of sectionalism is desirable, it follows at once that the president should be elected by a direct national vote. That would have the wholly desirable effect of emphasizing his national position. It would prevent the kind of fiasco which marked the Republican convention of 1912;[2] and it would diminish, as it is urgent to diminish, the excessive regard that is paid to the claims of the machines of both parties in doubtful states. The real truth is that, at present, the state as a unit of electoral refer-

[1] *The Significance of Sections in American History* (1932), p. 50.
[2] Cf. Pringle, *op. cit.*, pp. 561 f.

ence is wholly parasitic upon the party structure. To exalt its importance, as the present method of election does, is to give an entirely undue prominence to the type of man to whom "politics" is a profession in the worst sense of the word. It would do a good deal to eliminate candidates whose claims ought never to be considered seriously; and it would do something, at any rate, to save the remainder from commitments, both as to places and measures, they ought never to be asked to make.

Two further simple reforms are worth suggesting. I cannot see any case for the present limitation upon the president's veto power in finance. He must now accept or reject congressional measures as a whole. That means, despite the reforms of the budget, that he is still at the mercy of the "pork barrel" system with all its evil implications. I should like to see Congress adopt the kind of self-denying ordinance that has worked so admirably in the House of Commons; I would deny any member the right—the power of investigation apart—to ask for an appropriation that is not sought under the direct authority of the president. This would not merely result in more rational finance; it would also prevent the Appropriations Bill from being the plaything of perhaps a hundred members of Congress, whether in the House of Representatives or in the Senate, whose sole interest in finance is the local achievement in construction they can report back to their constituencies. This is a power already conferred upon the governors of many states, and, wherever it has been tried, there is no doubt that its effect has been beneficial.[3]

My second reform is also in the nature of a self-denying ordinance. Except upon purely selfish grounds, I can see no reason for the existence of "senatorial courtesy." It is rarely invoked except for narrow reasons; and, where it is invoked, its utilization is equally rarely defensible. Its effect is simply to narrow the area of presidential choice for ends intended not for the maintenance of a standard of appointment, but for the personal power of a particular senator. For reasons I have already urged, I think that the continuance of senatorial approval for the major nominations of the president is desirable; this approval would still remain. But it is wholly unfitting that a judgeship or a collectorship of a port should be dependent, as it now is, upon the effect it may have upon the balance of internecine interests within a section of the party in power. No one can seriously argue that "senatorial courtesy" is exercised to the end that bad nominations should be rejected; the well-known cases of Roscoe Conkling and Gallinger are evidence of that. No one, either, ought to ask a president so to use his nominating power as to assist men of the type of Ben Butler to build up a machine. It may be true that the power of individual senators would be adversely affected by this change. But it would not touch the collective power of the Senate. It would leave it free, in every case in modern times

[3] Cf. F. A. Cleveland and A. C. Buck, *The Budget and Responsible Government* (1920), and L. Lipson, *The American Governor* (1939).

in which its approval might reasonably be regarded as a matter of doubt, to resolve its doubts by debate. On the record, it is impossible not to feel that the dignity of American public life would be definitely increased if the Senate could be persuaded to accept this view.

"The fundamental addition which is necessary to enable the president to defy the pressure of local interests incarnate in senators and representatives," writes Professor Brogan,[4] "is the right to appeal to the nation by referendum. . . . The president should have an absolute veto over constitutional amendments proposed by Congress, until the country has decided between them, and the right to propose his own amendments, and his own direct legislation to the country, whether or no Congress approves. If it is possible to make national politics out of sectional politics, it can only be done through the presidency." I agree with the end Professor Brogan has in view; I cannot help feeling that his means are ill chosen. It is not merely that most of the issues upon which there is a division between executive and legislature do not seem to me susceptible of effective discussion by popular vote, and that this has been demonstrated by the history of the referendum in the various states;[5] it is also that the experience of the United States suggests strongly that the referendum is an instrument any frequent use of which would place excessive power in the hands of the most undesirable influences

[4] *Government of the People* (1933), p. 382.
[5] Cf. my *Grammar of Politics* (ed. of 1938), pp. 321 f.

in politics. I am confident, moreover, that many of
the issues so referred, that of the Tennessee Valley
Authority, for example—one of the half-dozen most
beneficent experiments in American history—would
be defeated by exactly that sectionalism that Professor Brogan is anxious to transcend. I doubt, further,
whether this right could be given to the president
without its conference upon the people also; and so
to extend that right would almost certainly in many
undesirable instances—the control of public utilities
is an obvious example—be to play directly into the
hands of the money power. The press and the radio
would be at the disposal of every evil influence which
had anything to lose. Who is there who cannot see
the kind of power such an occasion would give to
men like Mr. William Randolph Hearst or Father
Coughlin? And who is there who cannot see, also,
that the more indirect their influence over the voters
of the United States, the healthier and cleaner its politics are likely to be? The referendum is too blunt and
crude an instrument of authority to be of real use to
any president who is seeking an effective refreshment of power; and there is no reason to suppose that
an appeal to its power on the national plane could
ever be effectively canalized. A president might thus
be easily deprived of an authority he could exert in
one field because, by a narrow majority, and through
purely extraneous causes, he has suffered an accidental
defeat in another.

I am sure that Professor Brogan is right in his insistence that the transcendence of sectionalism is the

most urgent need in American politics; and I think he is probably right in arguing that the president is the instrument through which that transcendence may be most properly effected. The stronger the president, on the whole, the more likely it is not only that the attention of Congress will be directed to matters of general importance; but the more likely it is, also, that the mind of the nation will force Congress consistently to take that attitude. But to appreciate that problem we must, I think, probe deeper. We must consider what it is that has made the Congress so deeply a sectional body. It is not, I suspect, enough to say that it is so because American parties are inherently sectional. That only pushes the inquiry back to the further stage of what forces have made them inherently sectional. The answer to this complicated problem goes deep into the roots of American life.

For anyone who looks at the spectacle it presents will, I think, be struck at once by certain obvious things. It is, in the first place, clear not only that there is no "liberal" party in the United States, at least in the European meaning of that term, but also that so far no revolt from either of the major parties has had any real staying power. There have been many of those revolts; the Populist movement, the Progressive revolt under Roosevelt, the third-party movement under the elder La Follette, are only the most notable. But none of them has had importance on a plane of continuity. Sooner or later, their major figures either have returned, like Theodore Roosevelt, to the older parties from which they came, or have become politically impotent. It is notable, also, that except for brief periods, and in particular states, American labor has played no such part on the political stage as it has in European countries. It is striking that, so far, socialism has taken no hold at all of the American voter's mind; the economic crisis has deepened continuously since 1933, but the peak of socialist strength in the United States was reached in 1920, and even then it was, in proportion to the strength of the major parties, pitiably small.

These major parties represent, to a European, a curious spectacle. Though there have been moments when their differences upon particular issues were substantial, since the Civil War the dividing line between them has never been real. Grover Cleveland, for instance, might well have been a Republican president; and I cannot see any essential item in the program of President Hayes which an average Democratic president would not have been willing to commend. The truth is, I think, that these major parties have been essentially the agents of the property interests of the United States, that, in a general way, they have served them in much the same fashion, and that where they have diverged from service to them, it has been because of a profound popular agitation failure to respond to which would have meant electoral disaster. But up to, at any rate, the New Deal of 1933, the character of the response has always been within a very limited frame of reference which did not seriously disturb the conservative character of either of the parties. Within the limits permitted them by the

Supreme Court, they have been the legislative agents of business men and, to a less degree, the farming interests of the United States. The assumption upon which they have rested—the assumption, indeed, upon which the New Deal itself rests—is the social adequacy of American capitalism. They reflect its suspicion of government action. They represent the permanent desire of the man of property to be free from interference. Where they have been driven to interfere, it was usually either in a realm of minor importance or because crisis demanded a positive policy to which, at least immediately, they were compelled to give attention.

Anyone who considers the history of American parties until 1933 will, foreign policy apart, find a notable resemblance between their character and that of British parties before the advent of the British Labour party in 1906. They held a general social philosophy in common; they diverged from it only to make concessions to particular pressure groups whose demands would not brook denial. But they did not go beyond a fairly narrow frame of reference pricked out for them by the dominant property interests as sound. In a sense, indeed, they did not deserve the respect which the prewar parties in Great Britain were able to secure. Behind the congressional façade, both of them were unduly dominated by the great corporations and their representatives; it is still true of American politics as Woodrow Wilson quotes Dale of Birmingham as saying some sixty years ago that there is in the United States "a class, including thousands and tens of thousands of the best men in the country, who think it possible to enjoy the fruits of good government without working for them."[6] Whether the issue was the tariff or the trusts, railroads or electric power, taxation or the place of labor in the community, the parties were, subject to occasional revolts, in the hands of that "invisible government" of which Elihu Root spoke; a government of which the "bosses" were, as Lincoln Steffens so remarkably showed, more the symptom than the cause. The British aristocracy had, with all its limitations, a real sense of public service. The business aristocracy of America preferred to occupy itself with the making of wealth, leaving to the political parties the definition of the terms upon which it could be made, and themselves helping to frame those terms.

In this atmosphere, it is important ceaselessly to remember two things. First, the United States is essentially a continent; the making of unity out of its various sections was bound, therefore, under any circumstances, to be a difficult adventure. Second, because it was, until the nineties of the last century, a civilization in which expansion was always internal and not external, the creation of safeguards against discontent was a relatively easy matter. Opportunity, at least in comparison with Europe, was boundless; there was abundance of land, there was no residuary feudalism, almost any taxes produced a surplus in the treasury. Few members of the working class expected to remain there; most of them enjoyed conditions far

[6] *Congressional Government* (1885), p 331.

higher than anything the European peasant or industrial worker has ever known. The triumphs of the
business man were, on any showing, immense; in three
generations he had built a civilization out of a wilder-
ness. Up to the Civil War, there might have been
doubts and hesitations about the future of American
civilization; there were none after the issue of seces-
sion had been decided. From the presidency of Grant
onward, the United States seemed, to most, to have
made a permanent bargain with fate. The less positive
the action of government, the greater seemed to be the
tempo of its development. Parties, therefore, adjusted
themselves to an atmosphere in which weak government seemed the very condition of prosperity; and,
since the weaker the government the greater was the
leeway given to the power of the propertied interests,
the more jealously the latter scrutinized any movement toward regulation.

The real governors of the United States, that is,
wanted a weak system of rule. They were content
with an atmosphere in which, as Woodrow Wilson
said, "authority is perplexingly subdivided and distributed, and responsibility has to be hunted down in
out-of-the-way corners."[7] Every attempt at its concentration seemed unsound to the beneficiaries of the
system. It was "un-American"; it was an attack upon
freedom; it was contrary to the purpose of the
founders. And, in a fundamental sense, each of these
charges was true. For the concentration of authority
in American history has only been possible at mo-

[7] *Op. cit.,* p. 331.

ments of crisis. It has been accepted dubiously, and after the crisis has passed it has been discarded as rapidly as possible. The American people, trained in the tradition of negative government, have always been suspicious of it. That suspicion has been shared by Congress since the more strong the personality of the man in the White House, the more diminished has the authority of Congress itself become. From the foundation of the American system, the inference has been drawn that the stronger the president, the graver was the threat to public freedom. The men of 1787 could hardly help remembering, as they looked at the England they knew, that a legislature which could be dominated by the executive was the enemy of public freedom. They desired, therefore, "to erect a Congress which would not be subservient and an executive which would not be despotic."[8] They did so by a separation of powers which put a premium upon the possibility of governmental paralysis. "It was to have been expected that they should regard an absolute separation of these two great branches of the system (the executive and the legislature) as the only effectual means for the accomplishment of that great end."[9]

For something over a century they had every reason to believe that they were right. The system, on occasion, creaked and trembled; but, upon balance, within that period it resulted in a triumphant progress it is impossible not to admire. It was only after a century,

[8] Wilson, *op. cit.*, p. 30.
[9] *Ibid.*

when the epoch of abnormal expansion had begun to draw to its close, that analysis could suggest how real was the resemblance between the ends they had secured and the ends they had sought to avoid. For, having distributed authority, they found that, to cope with discontent, they had to bring it together again in order to prevent its paralysis. And the method by which the co-operation was secured bore a curious resemblance to the methods by which George III had made Parliament subservient to him. The use of the patronage by the president to obtain the majority he required was not very different from the use by George III of places and pensions to secure a majority in the House of Commons. The relation of the great interests to Congress has not been so unlike the domination of the eighteenth-century Parliaments to the interests of the great landowners. The truth of Lord Bute's well-known maxim that "the forms of a free and the ends of an arbitrary government are things not altogether incompatible,"[10] has been proved again and again in American history. And its truth has been emphasized by the way in which, from John Marshall onward, the Supreme Court has acted as a third chamber of the American legislature concerned to keep a possible co-operation between president and Congress within due bounds.

The spectacle of the separation of powers is, this is to say, the spectacle of the confusion of powers. A president may seek to give a lead; there is no one else in a position in which a clear lead can be given. But

[10] Cited by Woodrow Wilson, *op. cit.*, p. 308.

he cannot hope successfully to give a clear lead unless he is on one of two roads. He is likely to get what he requires if he takes what may be termed the retail view of his function. Whenever he does so, there is unlikely to be a great issue in dispute. He is then not challenging Congress for primacy in direction, and he may hope for success. He is likely, again, to get what he requires if on the path events compel him to tread the signals are set at danger. Then, at least, the prospect of a threat to the foundations of society leads to a co-operation in which he sets the direction. But, in all normal circumstances, the more positive a president sets out to be, the more unlikely is he to be able to insist upon his primacy. The whole drive of the system is against him. He is not only thwarting the separation of powers. He is also transforming the character of a party system which is, at its very basis, antagonistic to the idea of positivism. The American scheme of government is, in its inherent principles, not only a system for fair weather. It is also a system which, as it has translated itself into party terms, does not easily accept the categories of the positive state.

And this is the more important because America has now entered the epoch where the requirements of the positive state can no longer be denied. That can be seen from many angles. It is obvious, in the first place, because the dramatic period of internal expansion is over; the problems confronted by American capitalism are similar in character and intensity to those of Europe. It is obvious, in the second, because technological and scientific development have made largely obsolete the division of powers between the center and the circumference contemplated in 1787; in the epoch of giant capitalism only the federal government can hope to confront the great industrial empires on terms of equal authority.[11] It is obvious, in the third place, because the major parties have ceased to present the electorate with rational alternatives about any of the main problems to be solved.[12] That is the more emphatically the case because neither can admit within its ranks an organized labor movement seeking the translation of its needs into statutes on any wholesale scale. It is in fact evident that the labor problem in the United States is already—without its effective entrance into politics—forcing something like a realignment of parties there. Conservative Democrats and conservative Republicans find—as their attitude to revision of the Wagner Act made evident[13]—far more in common upon the basis of hostility to the claims of labor than they do in antagonism upon other issues. And what is true of their attitude to the labor problem is true, also, of their outlook upon most of the problems which the social policy of the "New Deal" has been called upon to solve.

The result can be put quite simply by saying that, emergency always apart, no president who has a positive policy to propound continuously will find, within

[11] Cf. my "Obsolescence of Federalism" in the *New Republic*, May 3, 1939.

[12] See this well put in Brogan, *op. cit.*, p. 383.

[13] On the Wagner Act cf. the admirable work of R. R. Brooks, *Unions of Their Own Choosing* (1939).

the major parties of today, any assured body of support for it. Something of what he may want he will get in the "honeymoon period" of his office; something, also, he may be able to extract by means of the patronage. But the more relentlessly he pursues major objectives that are positive in character, the more certain he is to find himself thwarted by the inherent nature of the party of which he is the nominal and temporary leader. If he gains a temporary respite with a view to renomination for a second term, he is likely to find increasing opposition as that second term draws to its close. As he disappears from the scene, he is likely to find himself replaced by a leader with whom the party can more comfortably deal on its own terms; it is not accident that a strong president has usually been followed by a succession of weak presidents, for they suit much better the environment to which both the American scheme of government and the American party system are historically conditioned.

2

America needs strong government; it needs strong leadership to attain strong government; only the president, granted its characteristics, can provide it with the leadership it requires. But against these needs must be set all the traditional impetus of the system. The Constitution makes against it partly by its separation of powers and partly by the way in which it has distributed functions between the states and the federation. It has now become of pivotal interest to the forces of privilege in the United States to maintain for their benefit both that separation and that distribution; and it must be remembered that, constitutional amendment apart, the degree to which that distribution can be effectively transcended lives precariously by the accidental composition of the Supreme Court.

The Constitution makes against it; so also, as I have argued, does the party system on its present foundation, since, except for emergencies, it enthrones the conservative forces in permanent power. These forces live by their ability to maintain weak government, for strong government, in the sense of a government with a continuously positive direction, is necessarily hostile to their interests. That can, I suggest, be seen from the intensity of their antagonism to the New Deal; they have greeted a body of legislation in general as mild as that of the Liberal government of 1906 in England as though it were inaugurating an epoch of red revolution. Since weak government is the source from which these forces draw their power in the state, their impact upon parties is always a discouragement to leadership in a positive form. And this discouragement can take many shapes. It may appear as sectionalism. It may appear through the frustration of the executive by an encouragement of opposition to its policies in the legislature. It may appear as the exploitation of the traditional American fear of strong government; there are few accusations to which the American public lends a more ready ear than to that of dictatorship, and that even when the very foundations of the system paralyze, almost a priori, any prospect of its constitutional advent.

I do not, therefore, believe that the strong leadership America requires will be available to it until the conflict between parties is on a rational basis; and I believe that this will require a radical realignment of parties. For where the choice between policies that has to be made is real, effective party discipline will follow the fact of the reality of the choice; and a president who is anxious to lead his party will then find that he has a party anxious to follow his lead. The problem, in fact, at least as I see it, is the adjustment of American parties to the disposition of social forces in the United States. At present, there is no such adjustment. Leadership on a big scale comes only because an emergency has to be surmounted. There is no provision for its continuity. On the contrary, the whole genius of the system is against its continuity. For once it becomes continuous, all the interests are weakened which suffer from its strength. A great president is bound to weaken them by the fact that he is great. I do not think it is true to say that he dwarfs his followers in Congress by the fact that he gives a lead. I do say that, by giving it, he makes Congress a unity behind him, for purposes he defines, instead of an incoherent mass of unco-ordinated elements which find their unity in the degree that they can alter those purposes. In the present scheme, the more Congress is able to defeat the president, the bigger it appears in the life of the nation. It is thus given a vested interest in his defeat. It is tempted to it by its inevitable and natural inclination to exalt its own stature. The Senator Robinson who carries out the will of the president will never appear so big a man in the eyes of the nation as the Senator Borah who successfully thwarts him. It is, in the present position, only human for most of those who go to Congress to have the ambition to be a Senator Borah rather than a Senator Robinson.

But a legislature is not of itself capable of positive leadership unless it is organized for this function. The British system organizes the House of Commons for this end by making it accept or reject, at the peril of a general election, the policies submitted to it by the cabinet. It does not lead the cabinet. It is not a policy-making body. It is an organ of registration, an instrument of criticism, a sounding board through which the voice of the nation can make itself heard. No provision is made for this relation in the American scheme. The president may urge his policies; he has no adequate sanctions to enforce them. And, once they are urged, he has no real certainty about what may become of them. There is no effective responsibility anywhere for their fate. An influential member of the legislature is, if he is of the majority party, as likely to have his way as the president; there are even spheres in which he is more likely to have his way. Congressional organization builds an executive within the legislature that is not truly charged with the executive function. Partly, it has the function of destroying the policy of the real executive; partly, it has the function of providing an alternative to it, which is rarely a part of any coherent pattern of policy. And the composition of this executive within the legislature is continually changing. It is one set of men on one set of problems; it is another set of men upon another. Whatever set of men it may be, one of their concerns must always be to establish and to emphasize their independence of the true executive power. But to establish that independence they must prevent his leadership from possessing that continuity of which I have spoken. They must, therefore, be a rampart against strong leadership. They must be a force to deny, not a force to co-operate in affirming. The purpose of the Congress, in the present scheme, must always be to make the presidency as weak as it possibly can.

This is not, I think, a situation that can be remedied by mechanical devices. I have already sought to show that it would not be cured by the introduction of a presidential right to a referendum. Nor do I believe, as has been suggested, that it can be cured by giving to the president a right to dissolve the Congress when they are at odds and seek, thereby, a refreshment of authority from the electorate. The implications of the right of dissolution are incompatible with the congressional system. They strike at the root of the separation of powers. The defeat of the president, at an election caused by its exercise, would obviously come very near to paralyzing his effectiveness during the remainder of his term; it is, indeed, doubtful whether, after such a defeat, he could usefully remain in office. And this is to say, I think, that the counterpart of a presidential right of dissolution is presidential responsibility to the new legislature he would so bring into being. If he were conceded that power, it would not be possible to avoid a rapid development of the parliamentary system, in something like the British form, in the United States. The presidential system, in its historic contours, could hardly survive the conference upon him of so tremendous a power without the exaction of a comparable responsibility.

I believe, therefore, that the changes required in the United States are likely to be produced less by direct constitutional innovation than by the repercussion upon the political framework of the immense social and economic changes that are going on before our eyes. This is not to say that I do not believe those constitutional innovations to be desirable. On the contrary, the case made, over seventy years ago, by Bagehot against the ultimate principles of the presidential system seems to me to have been strengthened, rather than weakened, by time.[14] But I doubt whether anything short of actual revolution would cause direct changes of the kind necessary to be made. The power of tradition is too great; the interests that could be mobilized against them are too strong. One has only to consider the relative failure of most efforts at direct innovation in the separate states, whenever the basis of the Constitution has there been called into question, to see how incomparably more difficult it would be to deal directly with the heart of the federal scheme. Revolution apart, it is to the pressure of usage and habit, as these are shaped by innovation within the economic fabric of the United States, that one must look for the main sources of change.

[14] Cf. my essay in *The Dangers of Obedience* (1930), pp. 31 f.

[248]

These innovations are on an immense scale; and they are likely to increase rather than to decrease in volume. It is not only that there is now a permanent proletariat in the United States with all the problems such a proletariat involves—permanent unemployment for a great army of citizens, services to mitigate its effects, and so on. Federal aid to states and cities is bound to grow, and as it grows the authority of the central government at Washington is bound to grow greater. A new level of social provision for citizens of low income in health and housing and education is inevitable; with them will come new levels and techniques of taxation intended, upon the European model, deliberately to effect such a redistribution of income as will mitigate the worst results of social inequality. All this is bound, I believe, to make the ambit of federal regulation in the future wider than it has been in the past. The state will be forced into an attitude far more emphatically positive than anything for which, so far, the "New Deal" has been responsible. There will be exacted, if American democracy endures, a much higher price for the maintenance of privilege than any it has so far been asked to pay.

It is worth while to insist, for a moment, upon the fact that there is nothing new or startling in this development. The critics of the "New Deal" speak of it as though it were a change of revolutionary intensity. The answer, to an outsider at least, is the simple answer that its roots are deep in American history. The "New Deal" of Franklin Roosevelt is the logical development of the "New Freedom" of

Woodrow Wilson. But this, in its turn, was the outgrowth of that Progressive movement of which the ambitions, perhaps, rather than the ideas, of Theodore Roosevelt made him the picturesque symbol. Yet no one can examine the Progressive movement at all carefully without seeing how much of it is rooted in Populism. This, in its turn, is a complex phenomenon the component elements in which go back not merely to agrarian discontent, but to a multiplicity of minor movements of protest the lineage of which is traceable to those things in the first days of the republic which made Shays a rebel and Jefferson president of the United States. All of them, I venture to think, were rooted in the effort of the ordinary man to get more from the common stock of welfare than he conceived himself to be getting, in the strong belief that he was morally entitled to more. All of them were more or less placated, sometimes by a recovery which transmuted demands for reform into silence, sometimes by immense grants of land, as under the Homestead Act, sometimes by those huge grants of pensions which have followed every military adventure in which America has been engaged. It seems to me, therefore, that unless there is old-fashioned recovery, on the nineteenth-century model, in the United States—and all the evidence suggests that this is no longer possible— the alternative of reform becomes inescapable. Reform means the positive state; and the debates of American politics in the next generation will turn on the pace and the quantum of the reform the propertied class is willing to concede or driven to accept.

From the angle of the presidency this has, I think, two implications. National politics in the next generation of American history will be far more important than in the past, because all the major problems of American economic life in the phase of giant capitalism project themselves, necessarily, on to a national plane. Whether the issue is the unemployed or housing, public utilities like railroads and electric power, the position of the farmer, the place of trade unions in society, the level and methods of taxation, they are insoluble problems if they are met in a sectional way. Their range and intensity will compel the political parties more and more to confront them nationally. The interests, above all that of labor, which will be forced by them into political consciousness, will, in their turn, compel a realignment of parties into conservative and progressive. Each of them will require, if it is to be effective in dealing, not merely with an electorate as vast as that of the United States, but also with one over which the power of organization is relatively small, a coherence and a discipline far greater than in the past. But to secure these, political parties will be compelled to centralize their leadership far more than they have before been willing to do. Centralization of leadership means, inevitably, a greater concentration of power in the president's hands simply because there is no other plane upon which it can be secured. He is likely, this is to say, to bear to his party a relationship far more like that of the British prime minister to his party than at any previous time. For his followers will find that, on the larger aspects of policy, the penalty of deserting the program he embodies is certain to be electoral defeat. In the America that is coming the penalty of electoral defeat will be far more important than it is today. That, above all, is why I think that the place of the president in the constitutional scheme is likely to be greater, his national authority even more immense, than at the present time.

3

This, obviously, raises a number of interesting questions, both of general and of technical importance. I take the former first, because it is easier to dispose of them. If, as I conceive, the presidency, in the future, is to be of more and not less importance than it has hitherto been, the question of the advice upon which the president can rely becomes clearly an urgent matter. The wider the range of his functions, the more profound the leadership he is called upon to give, the more, obviously enough, he must delegate; he cannot expect, in any considerable measure, to deal with any but the largest issues, or to do more than give general directions, to be fulfilled by others, in relation to all matters with the control of which he is charged. This, I think, raises the problem of supplying him with proper assistance, both on the political and on the administrative side.

On the political side, I think it means firstly a more important type of cabinet officer than he has generally had in the past. That is, in any case, desirable in itself; and it would be no more than a return to historic precedent, since the quality of the cabinets up to Jackson's day was far higher than it has been at any time since that period. The president of our own times has been too often satisfied with men upon whom he can rely less for counsel than for a purely personal allegiance, or with men whom it is desired to reward for services that are personal to himself, rather than political in character. He needs far more men of real standing, either because their influence in the party, as with Elihu Root under Theodore Roosevelt, removes from him a considerable part of the tremendous burden he has to bear, or because their past experience gives reason to believe that they will be the type of administrator who, knowing his mind, can be left a large discretion with safety. I think myself that this means a cabinet of men who are themselves of approximately presidential quality. It may be generally true that "a ministry of all the talents" is a difficult team to drive; it is certainly true that a ministry of little talent is one that it is broadly impossible to drive at all. The evidence is clear that, the weaker the cabinet, the more the president has continually to occupy himself with a mass of petty detail that ought to be quite below his notice. He does not delegate, because he is afraid of the results of delegation. He becomes his own head of department in a number of disparate offices to the functioning of which he is simply not able to give the requisite attention. Burdened in this way with oppressive detail, either he has no leisure to think in a large way upon the big questions, or, like Woodrow Wilson, he breaks down under the strain.

A president who is to function adequately needs a cabinet that is itself a training ground for the future occupancy of his position. On European experience, nothing compensates for the lack of this. It means leisure for the president. It means not only men who, in their respective spheres, can be largely left alone; it means also men who can be expected to ease his position with the legislature. This, in its turn, means knowing the legislature, and I think this involves the kind of experience of public life that high office, whether as a member of either house of Congress, or as the governor of a state, can alone confer. For, save with the very exceptional man, success in private life is not an adequate introduction to public office. The motivation of action is too different, the relation to other persons is too different also. It is not specialists in a departmental line whom the president requires as colleagues, but men who can take the kind of view he is compelled to take of the kind of problem with which he has to deal. The successful private lawyer—Mr. Ickes is a notable exception—can rarely think in this way; still less can the successful business man who is usually of little value in politics because that blending of wills in the give and take of compromise which is a large part of its essence is rarely a quality that distinguishes him. It is, above all, the quality the politician learns from handling matters of public responsibility. He comes to realize that words, there, are checks upon public account which there must be cash to meet, if credit is to be maintained. He learns, too, that decisions in politics differ from most decisions in private life, because they have to be defended with arguments that are certain to be attacked by the other side with all the resources at their disposal. That is why I think the cabinet of politically trained men will be indispensable to any president who is not himself so extraordinary that he could almost dispense with a cabinet altogether; and, Lincoln perhaps apart, there has been no such president in the history of the United States.

The kind of cabinet of which I am thinking is one upon which the president would be eager to rely for the definition of his general approach to his problems. I doubt whether any save the weaker presidents have had that reliance in modern times. The result has been either that they have striven to do too much, like Woodrow Wilson, or that, like Calvin Coolidge, just because they had weak counselors, they have been afraid to do anything at all. Mr. Coolidge's relation, indeed, to his secretary of the treasury, Mr. Andrew Mellon, is a supreme example of what the relation between a president and one of his cabinet officers ought not to be. Mr. Coolidge adored rich men because they were rich; and Mr. Mellon was one of the richest men in the United States. His conceptions of fiscal problems were antediluvian; and he had not the remotest idea of how to handle a legislature, a matter, indeed, of which he had no experience save indirectly through his relations with the Republican machine of Pennsylvania. But Mr. Coolidge assumed that a rich man must naturally make a successful secretary of the treasury; and the financial aspect of his policy as president was disastrous because he could not believe that, in the controversies between Mr. Mellon and Congress, the former could be wrong. A cabinet officer who had spent some years not, like Mr. Mellon, in obscuring his activities from the public, but, like Hamilton or Gallatin, in making his own views a matter of public conviction, would have been far more useful to the president. It is this type of man for whom he must seek; and, in a democracy, he is rarely to be found unless, at a comparatively early age, he has that direct experience of the art of public persuasion which is central to the achievement of the democratic purpose.

The reason, in a way, is not dissimilar from that which has made eminent naval and military men so unsuccessful in Great Britain—Lord Kitchener is the outstanding example—as ministers of the Crown. For the higher the office they reach in their respective professions, the more cut off they are from debate with other men on equal terms. No one can effectively argue with another man on his knees; and the soldier and sailor in high command have become so accustomed to the unquestioning acceptance of their views that they too seldom are accessible to that criticism which makes them state, and defend from attack, the groundwork of their basic assumptions. In the context of their cabinets, most presidents have been too much in this position. The men to whom they have been compelled to listen are too seldom independent men. In any case, the elevation of the presidency is so high that it does not make criticism from colleagues an easy matter; and, beyond this, there have been too many cabinet officers whose status had no significance in itself and except as office conferred it upon the particular occupant. That was, I may add, the inherent weakness of Colonel House's position in relation to President Wilson; his value ceased as soon as he chose to take an independent line. He was an intimate collaborator as long as he was content to be an echo; he was permanently estranged as soon as he tried to take a line of his own. A president, in the modern scene, who is likely to be successful must have about him men who are capable of taking a line of their own.

It is not, I think, an answer to this to say that the American Constitution makes provision for this necessity by the device of the separation of powers. For there is all the difference in the world between response to criticism which may be made without loss of prestige, and response which, if it is made, can at once be acclaimed as a partial surrender. The president's need is for men about him whose opinion on the general problems of his administration it is worth his while to hear, and this is a matter of finding men who are accustomed to expecting that attitude to their opinion and habituated to its formulation. Such men, as I have said, can be found in that broad category we call the public life of a nation. I do not think they can easily be found elsewhere, and because that is where they are most likely to be found, I suggest that, disregard being given to identity of general aims, their proper place is in the cabinet. A good cabinet ought to be a place where the large outlines of policy can be hammered out in common, where the essential strategy is decided upon, where the president knows that he will hear, both in affirmation and in doubt, even in negation, most of what can be said about the direction he proposes to follow. The evidence, I think, makes it clear that few American cabinets have been of this quality; they have not been a team of first-rate minds pooling their ideas in common. And until they become, by deliberate construction, as near such a team as it is possible for a president to make, he will not have at his disposal the basic human resources he needs to grapple with his formidable task.

This is a general problem: the choice of the statesmen who are to be the intimate collaborators of the president. But there is also a more technical problem in the choice of those personal subordinates who are to form his secretariat. It is an issue that is being increasingly discussed; it is one of which it would be difficult to overestimate the human importance. It is not precisely the problem of the cabinet secretariat in Great Britain, so happily devised by Mr. Lloyd George,[15] but of something that reaches beyond it. An efficient secretariat is the president's eyes and ears; it is also one of the most time-saving instruments at his disposal, and perhaps of all devices the president has most need of one that will save his time. A good secretariat has to take care that he is aware of all the currents and cross-currents of opinion amid which he has so delicately to thread his way. It has to see that the information he requires is instantly available when he

---

[15] On this cf. Jennings, *Cabinet Government* (1936), pp. 186 f. and my *Parliamentary Government in England* (1939), pp. 251 f.

requires it. It has to provide for him the contacts he ought to make and, not less important, safeguard him from those which are time-consuming without being significant. It must be able to provide him with at least the basic outlines of the public pronouncements he must make; a secretariat which cannot perform a good deal of the "ghost writing" a president requires on so immense a scale is, by definition almost, an ineffective secretariat. It must be able so selectively to deal with his massive correspondence that he sees its meaning in its relevant proportions; and it must give him that relation to it which so remarkably enabled Lincoln to make thousands of humble folk feel that their private problems were, in the public eye, a matter of presidential concern. It must have the faculty of self-suppression; and yet its members must, as persons, be significant enough to talk with authority in the president's name. They must not only know how to negotiate on his behalf; they must know what are the matters upon which they can suitably negotiate on his behalf. Without a secretariat capable of this function and at this level, it is pretty certain that the task of the modern president is infinitely more complicated and burdensome than it needs to be.

I think it is clear that no modern president has had a secretariat of this kind. Those whom they have chosen have, for the most part, been minor party hacks picked for their acquaintance with the party machine, or journalists who had not reached pre-eminence in their profession. John Hay was, indeed, for a time one of Lincoln's personal secretaries, and he appears to have played his part well. But such evidence as we have suggests that few presidents have really thought out at all seriously either the kind of secretaries they require or the function they ought to perform. The nearest approach I know to this effort has been that of President Franklin Roosevelt in the use he has made of Mr. Corcoran and Mr. Benjamin V. Cohen;[16] and it is interesting that a not inconsiderable part of the remarkable work they have done has aroused resentment rather than understanding. That resentment, perhaps, is not unconnected with the recommendation of the president's Committee on Administrative Reorganization that the members of the secretariat which they propose should have a "passion for anonymity." That is not, I fear, a possible ideal. Anyone today who is in the continuous service of the White House is, in the nature of things, news; their problem is less the "passion for anonymity" than the very different one of being able at one and the same time to deflect a reasonable amount of thunder and lightning away from the president without ceasing to be "available" for his purposes. If they succeed in doing that with skill and insight no one can say, granted the delicacy of the task, that they have failed.

The "passion for anonymity," indeed, deserves a separate word. If it is intended to connote the desirability of a secretariat whose ambition cannot be distinguished from the ends of the president, so that their own careers are subordinate to his purposes, it is, I

[16] For some account of their work see Joseph Alsop and R. Kintner, *Men Around the President* (1939).

think, an unexceptionable demand. If it is intended to mean that they should deliberately screen themselves from the public view, I believe that the end called for is not attainable, and possibly not even desirable. A dictatorship can afford, is even built upon, the *éminence grise*; and the history of Lord Esher reminds us that it is even compatible with constitutional monarchy.[17] But, in a democracy, I suggest that the more we know of the men who actually assist in the shaping of policy, the more honest that policy is likely to be. Those who do in fact shape it are pretty certain to be discovered; and it is better that they should be responsibly discovered than vaguely suspected. From the spring of 1938, for example, the rule of anonymity in the British civil service has helped to make of Sir Horace Wilson an omnipresent Machiavelli exercising an evil influence in every direction. I do not know what policies he has recommended, still less whether they have been wise or unwise. What, however, is clear is that the responsibility for action upon them is that of the British prime minister and his colleagues, and that Sir Horace Wilson has been fulfilling the role that is historically assigned to a civil servant of eminence in his country. That this role, and its performer, should be fully known is, I suggest, far better than that he should be the victim of every malicious quidnunc who can find a place for the deposit of his poison. In the end, that kind of speculation is bound to be injurious to the utility of any official who is its

[17] See his *Journals and Letters* (1934), 3 vols.; and my *Parliamentary Government in England* (1939), pp. 337 f.

subject. It prevents him from performing adequately those tasks that, under any circumstances, someone must perform. It offers the largest possible front to any intrigue against him, especially to illegitimate intrigue. So, certainly, it has been with Sir Horace Wilson. So, I think, it has been also with Mr. Corcoran and Mr. Cohen. Their only reward can be the confidence of the man they serve. But the way to preserve that confidence is by the public definition of their function. It can rarely be maintained if they are visualized as, so to speak, a class of administrative "G" men.

Such a secretariat as I have described is, I believe, an urgent necessity at the White House. It ought to act as a liaison between the president and the departments, between the president and the legislature, and, to some extent at least, between the president, the press, and the public. Its members will require ideas and imagination and discretion. Normally, they will need a good deal of experience in the ways of an administration; and this suggests at least the probability that a good deal of their value will be lost if they change with each president who comes into office. For I should judge from the available evidence that so far, most presidential secretaries have become really valuable to their chiefs just about the time when their term of office was drawing to a close. A man of extraordinary capacity can, no doubt, pick up the threads of this delicate task with exceptional rapidity. In general, its very range and multiformity makes it unlikely that this will be the case. It follows from this, I think, that an un-

changing personnel in such a secretariat is undesirable.
Men who have become habituated to a dozen years of
Republican rule like those from 1920 to 1932 will not
easily accommodate themselves to the exciting adven-
turousness of the New Deal. If they are to work usefully, accommodation to the presidential purpose, to
its mood and atmosphere not less than to its ideas, is
fundamental. This seems to me to involve a core of
permanence in the secretariat; the tradition and experience must be handed on from generation to generation. But it seems to me, also, to involve a need in each
president to supplement that core of permanence with
a small group of men whom he has himself chosen
because he feels that they are, in a special sense, his
own men. So organized, and working as a team—a
vital element in the whole situation—such a secretariat ought to be invaluable to a president. It could
see with his eyes and hear with his ears. It could perform a good deal of that incubation of ideas which
enables him to take up the threads of a problem mid-
way to its solution. No secretariat can ever make the
load of a president anything but grim and heavy; that
is the inherent price of being the president of the
United States. But, on these conditions, such a secretariat could do a good deal to make the load less intolerable than it now is.

4

Yet, after all, the main problem for the president is
his relation to that queer, shifting, labyrinthine amalgam we call public opinion. An average president is

likely to be a man in early middle age; Theodore Roosevelt, who became president accidentally at forty-three, is the only man, so far, to have attained the office under the age of forty-five.[18] He ought, therefore, to be at the height of his powers, old enough to have the maturity of experience, still young enough to bring energy to its interpretation. But, as he sets about his task, there are certain things he is constrained to remember. Most of the problems he will encounter are, in their ultimate foundations, shaped for him by the great, impersonal forces of past history; he will be able, proportionately, whatever his ability and energy and good will, to affect them in but a small way. He will be dealing with people who, on any showing, are mainly wrapped up in their private lives. They will find the bridge from their particular to his universal through the special interests of the environment in which those lives are enfolded. He will be dealing, too, with a people which is still externally, rather than internally, conscious of its unity, which can still be made only through a gigantic effort to think upon a national plane. Perhaps only two peoples, the Greeks and the British, have been more politically minded than the American; yet, to most of them, the drama of politics is compelling in an interstitial, rather than in a wholesale, way. Indeed, it is almost true to say of them that they are interested rather because things go wrong than because things go right. The harvest is so abundant that

---

[18] Pierce, Grant, and Cleveland were all under fifty on accession to office; the average age on accession is fifty-five.

prices fall; and the farmer looks suspiciously to know what the government proposes to do. The Stock Exchange is sluggish; and its votaries look around for presidential measures they may blame. The miners have gone on strike, and the winter coal supply is in danger; all eyes are turned on the White House to see how the president will tackle the threatened scarcity. The war clouds lower in Europe; what action will the president take to dispel them? Somehow, he has to transcend the hundred forces, the thousand voices, which compete to turn attention away from, or against, his central purposes. He has to seek the means of making men think his way, rather than another way. How far is it a possible task?

How far, moreover, is it a possible task in the light of certain facts that the observer is too prone to forget? He is president of the United States; but, in all probability, something like 40 per cent of the voting electorate has thought he ought not to be president, is ready, therefore, even eager, to be convinced that the case against him has been decisively made.[19] He is president of the United States; but a very considerable portion of those who voted for him feel that it is an essential part of his function not to compel them again to an interest in politics until the next time they have to vote. Thinking government always provokes a maximum resentment against itself, since the first thing upon which men economize is thought. He faces, too, on any showing, an opposition which will

[19] Cf. Holcomb in Logan, *The American Political Scene* (1938), Chap. 1 for statistics of voting in recent presidential elections.

exhaust all the resources ingenuity can invent, and money can buy, to represent all he does, and most of the things he does not do, in the worst possible light. He is president of the United States; but more people know intimately the habits of their favorite movie star, or the record of the outstanding baseball player of the season, than know the content of his policies. He is dealing all the time with those forces of tradition it is so difficult to move and so troublesome indirectly to circumvent. He is asking all the time, also, for an attention that demands effort, and often action, from people whose instinct it is to remain spectators, even aloof spectators, of the drama in which he is principal actor. "I am not interested in politics": is there any phrase more common in the discussions of our time? He has to deal with indifferent people and angry people, with the ambitious and the disappointed, with the cynical and the corrupt, as well as with those who are genuinely affected with a disinterested zeal for the public good. Only too often, he finds himself the victim of events he cannot control; the purpose he meant to be central becomes peripheral; the side issue becomes the fundamental theme. If he is always in a position to influence events, he cannot but remember that he is never in a position to dominate them.

Yet he starts with advantages that are important, if he knows now to capitalize them. For five months before his election he has been the central figure in the public attention. He has the opportunity to create expectancies. He has the power to compel discussion.

What he has to say, the very minutiae of his personality, will be the theme of talk in twenty million homes. Around him and his plans are a myriad hopes and fears. His problem is to maintain all he can of the tempo of those months. The answer to his problem lies in his having continuously something real to say, something positive and significant to do. The experience of the New Deal has shown, I think, decisively what an immense impact the personality of a president can make when he is able to arouse and retain the conviction that something of real importance is afoot. Whatever his effect upon Congress, a president who can get to the multitude will seize the attention of the multitude. His ideas, his policies, his purposes, will shape the mental climate as will those of no other man in America. He must, of course, be persistent in keeping them to the fore. He must see to it that they are not forgotten. He must persist; but he must never so persist that the public becomes fatigued with the debate in which he is engaged. He must convey the sense that the victory of his purposes is really of importance; and the best way to convey that sense is to fight battles in which both his supporters and his opponents alike feel that his victory really is important. That, it may be noted, has been the secret of much of the hold President Franklin Roosevelt has maintained over his electorate. He has gone for the big things; he has dramatized the issues upon which men know that their lives depend. He has communicated his own eagerness to those upon whose interest he has to rely. The enthusiasm of his supporters, the hate, even, of his opponents, have given a color to his term of office that has influenced millions to whom the spectacle is rarely of itself arresting. He has known how to prick men into thought, not least to prick the younger generation into thought. Because he has himself cared so much, he has made others care too.

That quality, it is important to note, has been characteristic of every significant president in the record. It is true of Jefferson, of Jackson, of Lincoln, of Theodore Roosevelt, of Woodrow Wilson. They were all positive presidents. They had a policy to recommend which seemed to their generation a challenge. Their supporters were, because of this, something more than the little regiment of professional politicians to whom the battle is significant for its spoils. They were, as in a war, an army of enthusiastic volunteers whose public interest in the outcome transcended their private inclination to aloofness. The leader's passion has communicated itself to his followers. He has aroused the dynamic of democracy, an energy, when it is aroused, more powerful and more pervasive than the dynamic of any other form of state.

This is, I think, the answer to the problem I have put. The president who can arouse this dynamic will make his policies a central thread in the life of the electorate. To do so, his effort must be a challenge. It must look forward and not backward. It must arouse a quality of interest that is essentially moral and positive in its nature. To end slavery, to curb the money-power, to build the "New Freedom," to establish, beyond peradventure, the foundations of the

"New Deal"—these make their appeal to the impulse of the crusader in man. The president who can do this penetrates within and beyond the little private life of the individual and links him, through himself, to purposes felt as great. There is an exhilaration in the atmosphere, a sense of big things on foot, which lifts the individual out of himself. Anyone who compares the fierce tempo of American politics under Jackson with that of his successors up to Lincoln, or of the age of Coolidge and Harding with that of Franklin Roosevelt, will, I think, have some sense of what this dynamic of democracy can imply. With the wisdom or unwisdom of the objects to which it is devoted, I am not, of course, here concerned. What alone is important is to emphasize this reservoir of energy to which an appeal is possible, the certainty, when it is aroused, that it will give to the president an authority over public opinion sufficient to make his purposes compete successfully with all other elements in the national life.

The challenge he makes must, of course, be one that is related to and expressive of vital human aspirations; without that relationship, it will rapidly run into the ground. Normally, it must be sufficiently within the framework of what the national tradition is seeking as to express purposes the common man is prepared to accept as a natural part of that tradition. A president so far ahead of his time as to voice aspirations the common man is not yet ready to understand is inevitably doomed to failure. The kind of challenge, this is to say, that he must make is one for which

[269]

history has already prepared a wide and secure foundation. It must seem immediately and recognizably desirable to a wide area of interests. It must, preferably, evoke attack from those who are widely felt to have been responsible for the need to make the challenge. From this angle, it is easy to see the significance of President Franklin Roosevelt's attack on Wall Street. Therein was implied not only a definite program of reform, the necessary emphasis, that is, upon positive aims; there was also implied the punishment of the men who were largely deemed responsible for the necessity of those reforms. In the first days of the New Deal, Wall Street could only have answered the challenge of the president had it been able, by the classic mechanisms of the free market, to overcome the gravity of the crisis. It would have had to establish recovery in order to stave off reform. Lacking the ability to do so, it transformed the reforming purpose into something akin to a religious crusade. It provided, the more it opposed reform, all the emotions of a drama in which each spectator felt himself associated with the fortunes of the actors involved. At its height, war and revolution provide that drama in its extreme form. In more normal times, the task of the democratic statesman is to elicit sufficient of the emotion to give the feel of great purpose in play, with sufficient of restraint to prevent the precipitation of conflict.

What I am seeking to say may perhaps be stated from a different angle. As soon as the American democracy moved into the epoch of the positive state,

it could not afford the luxury of dull government. [20]
For it is the inherent implication of dull government
that the dynamic of the national life is not profoundly
affected by its operations; and it is to the inherent
dynamic of the positive state that the operations of
government are profoundly important. From this it
follows that the government of a positive state must,
if it is to be successful, necessarily be a thinking government. It cannot function adequately either if, as
with Harding and Coolidge, it has presidents with no
ideas at all, or if, as with Mr. Hoover, it has a president whose fundamental philosophy is at variance
with its implications. The party struggle in the positive state can safely afford to be built upon a difference of opinion about the rate of change; it cannot
afford to be built upon a difference of opinion about
the direction of change. Once it is so built over any
considerable period of time the conflict between the
interests that are battling for power becomes too intense to be compatible with the democratic process.
The established expectations of men cannot then be
satisfied within the framework of reasoned discussion,
because one group will reject the assumptions upon
which the other builds. We have seen in our own
generation the outcome of such a rejection in Russia
in 1917, in Italy in 1922, in Germany in 1933, in
Spain in 1936. The positive state demands positive
parties; and positive parties demand positive pres-

[20] For the distinction between "dull" and "thinking" government
I am indebted to Bagehot, *Collected Works*, Vol. IX; but I fear he
would not have approved the use to which I have put it.

idents. That is the only way in which a democracy can be enabled to affirm its own essence; and a democracy that cannot affirm its own essence is compelled to the loss of its dynamic principle. When that period arrives, its downfall is always imminent.

Now what I have called thinking government is a far more difficult thing than dull government for two reasons. It is not only against more things in the past history of the nation—things, often enough, which tradition has made semi-sacred—it is also for more things in its future history. By the ambit of its affirmations, it provokes more denial than dull government is likely to do. It exacerbates public feeling; it arouses far more vivid emotions than ordinary men have known themselves to possess. Thereby also, it should be remarked, it is a far more educative process than its opposite; and, from this angle, it is far more in accord with the implied logic of democracy. But the inference I am anxious to draw from the fact that thinking government is a difficult process is that, the more urgently it is required, the less valid it makes that doctrine of "availability" which, so far, has played too considerable a part in the choice of presidential candidates. For if a man is to be selected on the principle of least offensiveness, he is likely, above all, to lack the positive qualities the modern president requires. A happy phrase of Mr. Robert Jackson, the attorney-general of the United States, puts with some precision what I have in mind. "I do not know," he told the Commonwealth Club of San Francisco,[21] "whether President Roosevelt is to have a third term; I do know that there must be a third term for the New Deal." Presidential candidates, in other words, must, increasingly, be capable of the kind of leadership the positive state and its problems require. "Availability," however charming, does not produce that kind of leadership. It destroys the possibility of thinking government. It makes for acquiescence in the given *status quo* of any epoch. It closes the avenues to significant change. It is, by its nature, against the future; and, because it is against the future, it is bound to dissatisfy the established expectations of the present. As the new America unfolds its possibilities, the party which stands by the doctrine of "availability" may win an occasional victory; but it will condemn itself, I think inevitably, to long periods in which it is eagerly excluded from power.

For the "available" president will have offered too many hostages to fortune before election to strike out a strong line of his own; his power effectively to lead will have been stricken into impotence before it has got under way. That will mean that while he is president the effective center of policy will be in Congress and not in the White House. That means, as I have sought to show, not merely that there will be no creative central direction of purpose; it means, also, by the nature of what Congress is, the service of sectional interest rather than the service—so urgently required —of national need. For, as I have argued, nothing but strong leadership from the president can give to Con-

[21] Speech of July 6, 1939.

gress the coherence and the responsibility it requires if it is to have that organic unity fit for the needs of the positive state. An "available" president means a weak president; and a weak president means a strong Congress. But a strong Congress does not mean a Congress united in determination of its direction. It means a Congress led in many directions by men whose particular purposes have never been fused into one strong and central purpose. A weak president, in a word, is a gift to the forces of reaction in the United States. It enables them to manipulate and maneuver between every difference that is provoked by the absence of a strong hand at the helm. It arrests the power to transcend the negativism which the scheme of American government so easily erects into a prin- ciple of action. A weak presidency prevents that transcendence of the limitations of 1787 which the compulsions of our generation demand.

It is not, I think, an answer to this argument to say that, if emergency requires it, the strong man will be forthcoming. The question rather is whether he will be forthcoming for purposes that are valid in demo- cratic terms. No doubt there is a real measure of truth in Bagehot's well-known aphorism that "the men of Massachusetts could work any constitution." When he wrote, his aphorism had far more truth in it than it has today, simply because the level of expectation from governmental action is so much higher than at any previous time. A constitution works well when men are in large agreement over the ends it should achieve; but their minds must be directed to the definition of those ends. And that there may be clarity in the direction, it is essential that there be leadership of a kind that no one but the president is in a position to supply. If he has the gift of leadership, if he has imagination, if, not least, he has the power, so supremely possessed by Lincoln, of understanding his fellow-men, he speaks in America from an unchallengeable eminence. Whatever voice is drowned amid the babel of tongues, his, granted these qualities, can always be heard. Even today there are phrases of Washington and Jefferson that remain a constant part of the national tradition; and some of the more vital of their gestures shape the habits to which all Americans must conform. Lincoln's brief utterance at Gettysburg has transcended all national boundaries; and wherever a civilized tradition remains, its echo still lives in the minds and hearts of men.

So, with great leadership in the president, it can continue to be with the American nation. If their problems are immense, so also is their promise. Their resources are still vast. There is absent from their lives the weight of that feudal tradition which still bears down so heavily upon Europe and Asia. They are an experimental people, restless, alert, energetic, in a degree that is rich with hope. They confront, no doubt, new issues in a setting far different from any that could have been conceived by the fifty-five men who gathered together in that summer of 1787 in Philadelphia. Science and technology have annihilated their isolation from the Old World. Their freedom is jeopardized, as so much of our freedom in England is jeopardized, by their servitude to the past, by the tribute they pay to a privilege which, there as elsewhere, exacts its full meed of claim. But in America, as in no country save one in the world today, there are the two supreme possibilities of exhilaration and hope. With them, too, has come a new maturity and a new seriousness. More people are aware than ever before that institutions are made by men for the service of men, that they live as they are adapted to larger ends. More people, too, realize that the form of a constitution is a dead and inert thing save as it is inhabited by the quick spirit of men eager to make it serve planned purposes of a nobler design. A nation that wills to be free must, as it is there increasingly understood, see its traditions not as chains but as opportunities. To live creatively, it must discipline itself to trust, in the grand manner, the leaders of its choice.

No office in the world today carries with it greater responsibilities than the presidency of the United States; its holder needs the confidence of those who have elected him in full measure if he is to fulfil those responsibilities. He needs criticism, too; the knowledge that comes only through the expression of criticism of the grievances that are felt, the needs to which he must respond. But above all he requires, in a fuller measure than ever before, the chance to lead his people forward. If he has a duty to his people, not less is its duty to him. From it he must expect the renovation of faith in his purpose, the demand that he does not falter in setting that purpose high. Above all, for the refreshment of that faith, he must look to the common man. For it was the central purpose of the American dream to assuage his sufferings and to enlarge his prospects; it was its central purpose to make possible a genuine freedom for the many and not a privileged license for the few. As no man in the Western democracies, the president of the United States can lead in the task of giving reality to that dream. To do so he requires courage and ideas; to do so, too, he must be given the power adequate to his responsibilities. He is waging a war, as he fulfils his purpose, against those who, as Franklin Roosevelt has said, "have conceded that political freedom was the business of the government, but . . . . have maintained that economic slavery was no one's business. They granted that the government could protect the citizen in his right to vote, but they denied that the government could do anything to protect the citizen in his right to work and his right to live."[22] As a people permits the power of a propertied class to insist upon that denial, it embarks upon the road that leads, in the end, to tyranny.

Power, no doubt, is always a dangerous thing; and the temptation to its abuse, as no generation has learned more surely than our own, the subtlest poison to which a man may succumb. Yet power is also opportunity, and to face danger with confidence is the price of its fulfilment. That is why I end with the emphasis that the president of the United States

[22] *Public Papers and Addresses* (1936), V, 233. Speech on the acceptance of the renomination for the presidency.

must be given the power commensurate to the function he has to perform. It must be given democratically; it must be exercised democratically; but, if he is to be a great president, let us be clear that it must be given. With all its risks, its conference is the condition upon which the American adventure may continue in that form of which its supreme exponents have most greatly dreamed. To withhold it, or to frustrate its ample operation, is to jeopardize that adventure. For great power alone makes great leadership possible; it provides the unique chance of restoring America to its people.